IMAGES
of America

ZELLWOOD

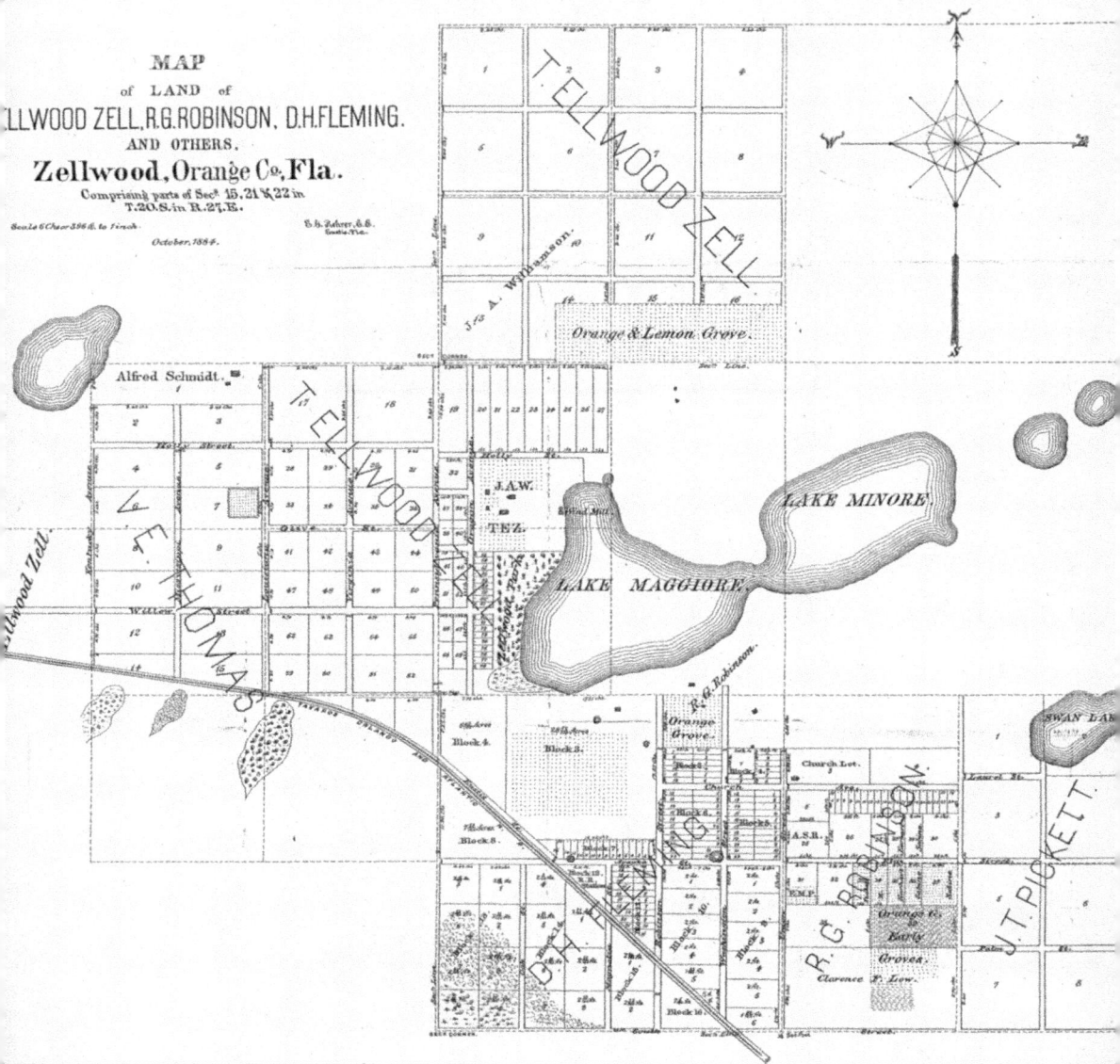

This 1884 map of Zellwood shows sections of land owned by Thomas Zell, Richard Robinson, and Daniel Fleming, as well as other owners listed in Zell's scrapbook. Fleming's land contained the depot, businesses, homes, Taylor's planing mill, Mrs. Dunn's boardinghouse, Mitchell's boardinghouse, H.H. Ashman's store, and the office of local physician Dr. Charles Lanphear. The areas owned by Robinson and J.T. Pickett contained residences and groves. (Courtesy of John Maseman.)

ON THE COVER: Around, 1921, Thomas Edward Newton purchased property diagonally across from the Zellwood Inn, and by 1924, he had built this home. Pictured here are, from left to right, (first row) Bernice, Gertrude, and Ruth Wilkins; (second row) Velma Newton and her mother, Rachel Newton; (third row) Bernard D. Wilkins, Thomas (Rachel's husband), Elsie Pearl Newton Wilkins, and George Newton (brother of Elsie and son of Thomas and Rachel). (Courtesy of the Wilkins family.)

IMAGES
of America

ZELLWOOD

Zellwood Historical Society,
Museum, and Library, Inc.

ARCADIA
PUBLISHING

Published by Arcadia Publishing
Charleston, South Carolina

Library of Congress Control Number: 2014931059

For all general information, please contact Arcadia Publishing:
Telephone 843-853-2070
Fax 843-853-0044
E-mail sales@arcadiapublishing.com
For customer service and orders:
Toll-Free 1-888-313-2665

Visit us on the Internet at www.arcadiapublishing.com

*To the many unique individuals who settled in and
founded Zellwood—land speculators, hunters, fishermen,
farmers, citrus growers, nurserymen, shopkeepers,
businessmen, laborers, and all other Zellwoodians.*

CONTENTS

ACKNOWLEDGMENTS

This book was inspired by Charles E. Grinnell Sr., a Zellwood farmer. We are grateful to the Zellwood Historical Society and the friends of Zellwood who provided photographs and information to complete this project. The Zellwood Historical Society would like to thank Marjorie Grinnell, Jack Humphrey, Deloris Brown Lynch, Rosa Lee Ondich, Denny Shiver, and Cicily Vincent Turner for their work on this book. Liz Gurley, of Arcadia Publishing, encouraged and guided us. William Lovelady, of D&L Publishing Group, and Nicole Lovelady provided technical and editorial assistance. Our friends at the Museum of the Apopkans have supported us throughout the process. Zellwood Community Center provided workspace. George Kluhsmeier helped establish the Zellwood Historical Society, which yielded archival records and photographs. The Leon and Violet Osborn collection (OC) was a source of images and unpublished information. The invaluable publications we consulted include the following: *The Apopka Chief*; *History of Apopka and Northwest Orange County Florida*, by Jerrell H. Shofner; and *Countdown for Agriculture in Orange County, Florida*, by Henry F. Swanson.

All images appear courtesy of the Zellwood Historical Society, Museum, and Library unless otherwise noted. For providing additional images for this book, we thank the Lovelady family (WL), Janice Fly Blackwelder (JFB) (for the King and Fly family photographs), the Charles Grinnell Sr. family (CG); and Cicily Vincent Turner (CVT).

INTRODUCTION

No soul remembered is ever really gone or forgotten.

Via these pages, the Zellwood Historical Society, Museum, and Library remembers Zellwood's beginnings, its people, and its events.

A traveler, lulled by the monotonous clip-clip-clip of the highway as he zips along Orange Blossom Trail from Orlando to Mount Dora, might not realize he has passed the Conquest Cemetery or the Laughlin historic district, or driven within two miles of Sydonie, one of Orange County's historic buildings. Who would guess that one mile south, there were once muck farms that helped feed the nation? Or that Native Americans left dugouts and arrowheads on the north shore of Lake Apopka? Do the motorcyclists who park by the two-story wooden building realize that it was once a trading post—that it is one of the oldest commercial establishments in Orange County?

Travel with us down memory lane.

William Carter Goolsby migrated to the Zellwood area around 1850. With the help of slaves, he cleared land, planted citrus groves, and constructed buildings along the edge of Lake Apopka in Grassmere, which is now the area known as McDonald. In nearby Conquest Cemetery are the Goolsby family's headstones, among others, and unmarked burial sites of slaves. The Goolsby and Wilkins families built Conquest Methodist Church near the cemetery.

With the development of the railroad in the late 1880s, more people arrived in Zellwood. The Vincent, Vine, and Morton families, along with a cattle car hired by the group of families, arrived from Texas via train in 1911. Supplies came in; citrus and vegetables were shipped out. Telegraph service was available, and trains brought word of weather from the north.

The early settlers found this area to be beautiful with its lush growths of oak and pine trees and palmetto and sable palms—all covered with vines and moss. Wild blackberries and huckleberries were plentiful, providing pioneer women with ingredients for jellies, jams, and pies. Adjusting to their new lives may have been hard for these refined ladies, who relocated to Zellwood from the north to live in somewhat primitive conditions while waiting for their homes to be built. The earliest pioneers did their cooking outside on an open fire.

Settlers around Lakes Maggiore and Minore included publishers, doctors, lawyers, judges, real-estate salesmen, and retired military officers. These were intellectual, cultured, well-read, and successful people. Housing was needed, so families accepted boarders and built inns. Homesteaders constructed houses from trees found on their land. Over time, Zellwoodians built homes from available resources, including disassembled buildings. Inexpensive shelter—including Army barracks and Wilson Cypress Lumber Company camp houses—was relocated to Zellwood. Socioeconomic groups ranging from extremely wealthy folks to farm laborers made their homes in Zellwood.

Some early citizens were attracted to Zellwood because the climate was ideal for growing citrus, peaches, and pineapples. These endeavors were successful until the big freezes of 1884 and 1885. During one of the freezes, Richard Robinson attempted to save his citrus trees by burning the fence surrounding his grove.

An influx of people during the 1940s caused a growth spurt in Zellwood's population. During this time, the Sewells, Barretts, Smiths, Bryants, Millers, Humphreys, Browns, Willifords, Grinnells, and Shivers came to Zellwood to start businesses or find work. Many migrated from Georgia and found employment in the citrus and farming industries. Some over those who arrived in the 1940s may remember waking up to the hum of crop-dusting airplanes flying over the farmland, smelling the fragrance of orange blossoms in the air, and picking fresh oranges to eat.

On summer afternoons, families went for a swim in nearby Lake Ola or Rock Springs. A trip to the Sanford Zoo was a huge event in a child's life. Daytona Beach beckoned people to drive over and enjoy the sun and surf. Teenagers traveled to Daytona early on Saturday mornings and parked in front of the boardwalk to hear the hit songs of the day coming from the loudspeaker.

Businesses provided work opportunities and improved the local economy. The Jones & Lovelady grocery store, Stewart's Sundries, various produce packinghouses, and plant nurseries offered jobs. Adults and teenagers appreciated the opportunities to earn; it was a privilege to be hired, because jobs were scarce in Zellwood.

In the 1950s, the residents of Zellwood began to advocate for better living conditions. Frame houses were erected on little dirt and clay roads. Some families living close to each other would trust an aunt or matriarch to watch the children; while parents were away at work, this responsible person would visit each home to help the children do laundry or cook the evening meal.

Children called the roads either dirt roads, clay roads, blacktop roads, or hard roads. In the late 1940s, the city elected a Corn Queen—a penny counted as one vote, and all of the contestants wore wrist corsages from Vincent's Florist. Barbara McCall was crowned at Rock Springs after her employer put a sizable bill in the penny jar, which put her over the top. The Youth Center on Union Street served as a meeting place for the town, as it still does today. Many citizens donated labor and/or money to provide a place for the youth. Many events, like plays and graduations, have been held on the stage. The Youth Center is now known as the Zellwood Community Center. It has long been the scene for quinceañeras, birthday celebrations, anniversary parties, and community reunions.

Zellwood residents' fond memories include the huge oak tree beside Lenny's drugstore, which he lit with 60-watt colored lightbulbs each December; the Christmas lighting in the community was simple but beautiful to a child's eyes. Children played outside and were quite creative when entertaining themselves. Some would pretend they were in the Army, especially if their fathers had been in the war. Many men were shade-tree mechanics on the side, and if dad was not looking, the kids would play in the cars, pretending to go on trips their parents had talked about. Youngsters officiated many animal funerals in those days, gathering under the oak trees for the services and singing the songs they had heard in church. They loved to go to W.D. Lovelady's store to get penny candy and all-day suckers. The best beef around was sold at Lovelady's, and there was nothing like a piece of cheese cut off the big, round, wax-covered wheel. School buses took children to the fair each year, leaving at 9:00 a.m. and returning at 4:00 p.m. Some of the kids would spend their money by noon and then wander around for the rest of the day in the exhibit area, hoping for the bus to return early.

Regrettably, there were no photographs in the archives of the Zellwood Historical Society showing Frederick Douglas School, early times on Willow Street, and other aspects of Zellwood's history that deserve to be remembered. However, within these pages, we share images intended to provide a peek back in time—and possibly to reveal a few surprises.

One

ZELL AND EARLY ARRIVALS

Zellwood's namesake, Lt. Col. Thomas Ellwood Zell, arrived in 1876 and stayed at Lichen Place. On return trips to the area, the Zells wintered with John A. Williamson for several years until their home was completed. They homesteaded 160 acres northwest of Lake Maggiore and planted citrus. A colony of retired Army officers, lawyers, and doctors was established near Zell's two-story home. Zell died in Zellwood in 1905, and he was later buried in Philadelphia. (Courtesy of John Maseman.)

Old williamson House when we first came to Zellwood 1911

The J.A. Williamson family left Philadelphia via steamer and headed to Jacksonville. They traveled the St. Johns River to Sanford and then came 30 miles over land. They arrived in Zellwood on October 28, 1876. The Williamson family stayed with a Mr. Neal in Grassmere during construction of their home. They hosted religious services, theater shows, and social dances. Newcomers to the area would often stay with the Williamsons until their homes were erected. (JFB.)

Lt. Col. T. Ellwood Zell erected one of the most substantial and costly homes in Zellwood on the northwest corner of Lake Maggiore. He liked the topography of the land and the climate, which reminded him of Italy and was suited for growing vegetables and fruit. Zell entered 160 acres for homestead, practically surrounding the lake. He later learned he could preempt another 160 acres at the west end of the lake in the name of his brother-in-law, John A. Williamson. The two formed a partnership and began to make their fortune growing citrus trees. Records indicate that this house belonged to either Zell or Williamson.

10

Lt. Col. T. Ellwood Zell was the owner of a publishing company in Pittsburgh, Pennsylvania, and contributed books to the Zellwood Library. The donated books include the nicely illustrated *Descriptive Hand Atlas of the World*, by John Bartholomew. Another donated tome, *Zell's Encyclopedia*, illustrated with woodcuts, is dated from 1871. (Courtesy of Hannah Brown Bloser.)

Capt. Charles Sellmer was one of many Army officers who helped establish a colony in Zellwood after T. Ellwood Zell settled in the area. Sellmer bought property from Zell, later retiring and moving his family south. He grew citrus trees and engaged in the real-estate business. Sellmer's property, located on Washington Street near Lake Maggiore, had a 20-acre grove and gardens. (OC.)

The settlers of the lake region of Orange County found land covered in tall pine trees, hammock thickets, palmettos, vines, and oaks with Spanish moss. The lake water was clear and clean. The settlers would homestead a piece of property and cut down the giant pines for lumber to build homes and businesses. Nearby mills processed the lumber used for construction.

This photograph, from an album showing scenes around Laughlin Estate, shows the view from Washington Street's terminus at the south shore of Lake Maggiore.

William Braxton Bragg Hammond (left) called Zellwood home for a while after his wife, Mollie Evelyn McFarling Hammond (right), died in 1900. Hammond's farm produced poultry, vegetables, oranges, ferns, and pineapples. He often relocated to build sawmills in various timbered areas, creating villages with a commissary, homes, and a schoolhouse near the mills. In 1902, Hammond married young Margaret McQuaig. (Both, courtesy of Frankie Hammond.)

To provide employees and their families with easier access to necessary supplies, commissaries were erected near remote timber-cutting operations. In 1900, William Hammond, a dealer in rough and dressed lumber, owned this commissary and an orange grove. Hammond shipped fruit to family in Alabama for them to sell. The workers shown in this c. 1902 image are, from left to right, Joe Carter, Jeff Harding, John W. Hammond, and A. Caldwell. (Courtesy of Frankie Hammond.)

Lilla Hammond (left), the daughter of Mollie McFarling Hammond and William B.B. Hammond, married Lewis Cass Osborn (right). Their children were Leon, Ralph, Wallace, and twins Ruth and Rufus. Lewis and his brother, Charles, co-owned Osborn General Merchandise with their father, Caleb Osborn. Caleb purchased the business, located on Jones Avenue, from Herbert Ashman in 1889. Lewis was appointed Zellwood's postmaster on July 27, 1911, and served until his death in 1928. (Courtesy of Frankie Hammond.)

Lilla and Lewis Osborn stand on either side of an oak tree in this c. 1913 photograph. Lined up in front of the fence are four of their five children. The older woman standing behind the children and the older man standing to the left of the car may be Lewis's parents, Mary Ann Jones Osborn and Caleb Osborn. Caleb died in August 1913, and Mary died in 1922. (Courtesy of Frankie Hammond.)

A trading post supposedly existed as early as 1886 in the area where George W. Foote constructed this building as his home in 1888. The property was later owned by Herbert H. Ashman. In 1894, Caleb Osborn purchased it, and he ran Osborn General Merchandise in partnership with his son Lewis. An added section served as the post office, and the building also contained a library.

In this 1904 photograph, Lewis (seated) and Lilla (holding baby Leon) Osborn pose on the porch of their home in Zellwood. Lewis's mother, Mary Ann Jones Osborn, is seated at right. The other two women are unidentified but may be Lewis's sisters. (Courtesy of Frankie Hammond.)

In 1884, Edith Fairfax Davenport arrived in Zellwood with her father, Judge Joe K. Davenport, after traveling from Kansas City, Missouri. The family built a home on Lake Maggiore. This image shows Davenport with her Sunday school class in 1910. (OC.)

An artist of distinction, Edith Fairfax Davenport received her education while residing in Paris, France, and Florence, Italy, for 12 years. She is listed in *An International Dictionary of Women Artists Born Before 1900*. Davenport received many awards for her art. As a cousin of the artist James McNeill Whistler, she was granted special permission to paint a copy of his original, *Arrangement in Grey and Black No. 1* (commonly known as "Whistler's Mother"). J.W. Paul and Davenport instituted the Zellwood Free Public Library (later called Zellwood Public Library) in 1912. Davenport was devoted to the library and established a fund to keep it operating. The photograph at right shows Edith Davenport (left) and Byron Morton McCoy (second from right) at the beach. (OC.)

Encouraged by Jones Vincent, who had already settled in the area, the Vincent, Vine, Pugh, Morton, and other families chartered a passenger train car and two cattle cars from Waxahachie, Texas, in December 1911. After these families arrived in Zellwood, they became the backbone of the community. They came to make a living on the muck farms—first by growing potatoes, then by selling dehydrated peat around the United States and Europe. Members of the Vincent family became pioneers in the fern industry. (CVT.)

Fredonia Vincent (pictured) was among those who stepped off the train in December 1911. She later married Tildon Pugh, and the couple had a son, Carroll Pugh. Carroll was born in Sydonie, the main house on Laughlin Estate, in 1915. Carroll and Lillian Ann McLucas married and had two daughters, Mary Frances and Carol Ann. (Courtesy of the Pugh family.)

This 1914 portrait shows Maude and Leo Stenstrom at the Passmore home on Ponkan Road. Joseph and Elizabeth Passmore were Maude's parents. Maude and Leo had two children—Josephine and Leon. Josephine married Earl White, and they had two children—Marvin "Skeet" and Ann. Leo was the town barber, working from a building behind Caleb Osborn General Merchandise. He relocated to a spot beside Cliff Bateman's café and general store and, in later years, worked from his home on Union Street. (Courtesy of Skeet White.)

In Ohio, during the spring of 1911, the Slavia Colony Company—a group consisting of Lutherans of Slovak descent—sought desirable environments for members who were unhappy living in industrial areas; the company wanted to help members relocate to agricultural areas. The Slavia Colony Company hired three scouts, provided capital for the scouts to purchase land in Florida, and resold the land to members on affordable terms. While searching for suitable land to purchase, the scouts photographed this Slovak settlement in Zellwood on March 28, 1911. Oviedo, located 30 miles from Zellwood, was to the scouts' liking, and they purchased land there. The part of Oviedo where Slovaks settled became known as Slavia. The Slovaks living in Zellwood and Slavia interacted because of their cultural commonalities.(Courtesy of Archives of St. Luke's Lutheran Church, Duda Family Collection.)

Two

COMMERCE AND TRANSPORTATION

Reasley W. Vincent Sr. shows off the Vincent family car in this c. 1920 picture. At the time, there were only two cars in Zellwood. Vincent sold J.R. Watkins products throughout Zellwood and the surrounding area from the backseat of the car. The family—especially the youngsters!—enjoyed the entertaining outings he provided in his automobile. (Courtesy of the Vincent family.)

The Zellwood Inn sign along Orange Blossom Trail pointed guests to the inn at the southeast corner of Washington and Church Streets. Fried chicken, biscuits, and stewed apples attracted diners to Elizabeth Letsinger's table. She and her husband, Elijah, had arrived from Tennessee by train in 1910. The original Zellwood Inn (above) was completed in 1911, but it burned down in 1923; Tom Morton built a new inn (below) in 1925. After Elizabeth's death in 1946, the inn briefly closed. Robert Edward Letsinger, Elizabeth's grandson, along with his mother (Helen), his wife (Ruth), and staff, soon again opened it. In its heyday, the Zellwood Inn served many guests. The 1940s brought men who had come to farm on Zellwood's muck land and boarded at the inn. In the late 20th century, the inn became a private home. (Both, courtesy of the Letsinger family.)

Elizabeth Letsinger operated the Zellwood Inn until she was 78 years old, offering as many as 18 varieties of food served family style. She took the train to Leesburg for provisions and raised vegetables in her own garden. Wild cows and snakes plagued her as she made her way to the train depot or tended her garden. The inn's guests included Richard Whitney, who was experimenting with growing ramie on the muck land. (Ramie was a hemp-like plant which, upon processing, would yield a durable fabric.) Albert T. Hartcorn stayed at the inn while his Holly Arms hotel was being built. Elizabeth's daughter-in-law Helen Letsinger (center) welcomed guests to the table at the Zellwood Inn. (Courtesy of the Letsinger family.)

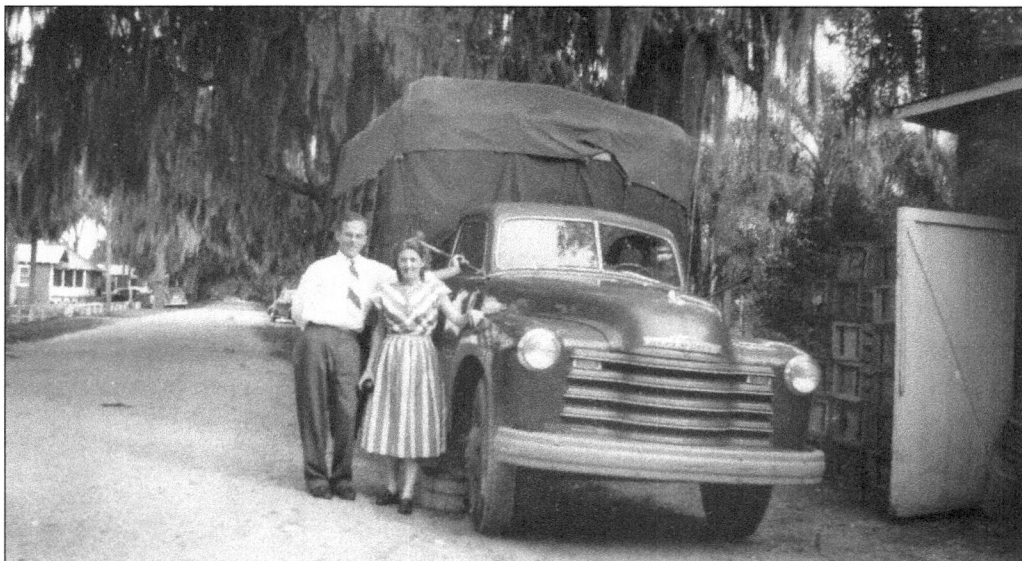

Robert "Bob" Letsinger ran a produce business on the Zellwood Inn property. Here, he and his wife, Ruth, stand by their red two-ton Chevrolet on King Street. Letsinger Produce brought fresh fruits and vegetables directly to the inn and also traveled throughout Florida to deliver produce grown by Zellwood farmers, including those with the last names Clonts, Duda, Lust, Long, Grinnell, Gerwig, Stewart, and Jorgensen. (Courtesy of Robert Earl Letsinger.)

The Holly Arms, owned by Albert T. Hartcorn, was built around 1915 at the northwest corner of Jones Avenue and Laughlin Road. The 1916 *Official Hotel Red Book and Directory* listed its rooms as costing $2 per night. The lobby contained a telegraph and money-order office. Richard Whitney bought the hotel to use as a hunting lodge and built a 50-by-20-foot concrete swimming pool. The Regina music box in the lobby was quite an attraction; a patron would select a metal disk, wind the handle, and hear beautiful music (mostly waltzes). Franklyn and Geraldine Gaede lived at the hotel while establishing Ohio Farmers, a business co-owned by Franklyn and Andy Couch, who grew radishes in Zellwood and also had a farm in Ohio. Michael Ondich Jr. owned the Holly Arms from 1946 until 1972, when he sold it to Zellwin Farms. The hotel burned down in the mid-1980s. (Above, courtesy of Adelbert Raulerson; below, courtesy of Rosa Lee Ondich.)

The HOLLY ARMS, ZELLWOOD, FLORIDA

The building that housed Osborn General Merchandise, the post office, the Masonic lodge, and the library became the hub of social activity. Fancy balls and dances held upstairs attracted people traveling by train from as far away as Orlando. Bands—complete with harps—also arrived by train. These events were long-gloved affairs. James Leroy Giles, a clerk employed by Lewis Osborn at Osborn General Merchandise, went on to be elected mayor of Orlando three times. The upstairs of the general store was converted into apartments in the 1940s, providing housing for families, including the Brantleys, Tuckers, and Browns. After the Masonic Order joined the Apopka Lodge, Lewis Osborn and L.F. Stewart would ride together to the meetings in Stewart's Maxwell car or Osborn's ancient Cadillac. (JFB.)

Around 1947, the Bee Hive apartment house on the south side of Highway 441 caught fire when something on a stove ignited. The building, owned by E.W. Fly, had been moved from an Army base. It was called the Bee Hive because the active children who lived there seemed as busy as bees. Allen and Sally Sewell, Dot and Jim Goodman, and the Ryals and Browning families were among those who once lived at the Bee Hive. (CG.)

Lester Brittian Vincent poses with examples of his outstanding taxidermy. He was locally known for his talent for realistically preserving wildlife in the workshop behind his flower shop. Hunters brought their trophies to Vincent to be preserved. His considerable artistic talents were showcased in both his taxidermy and his flower business. (Courtesy of Becky Vincent Juvinall.)

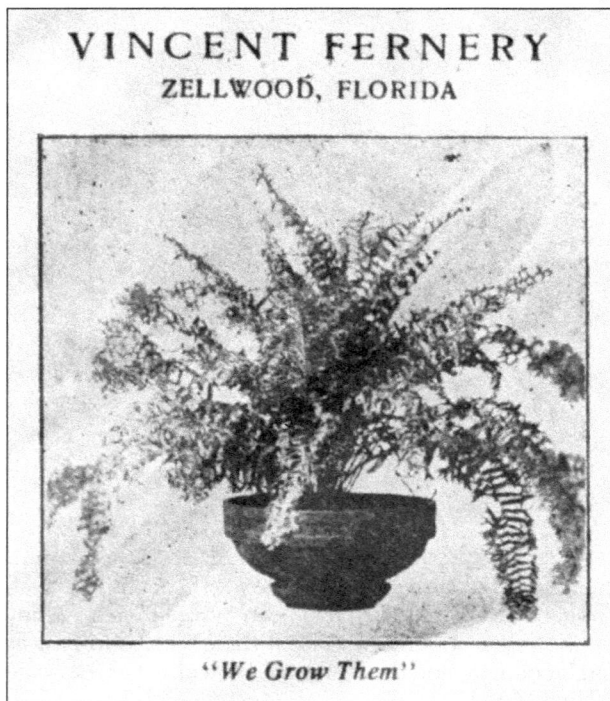

VINCENT FERNERY
ZELLWOOD, FLORIDA

"We Grow Them"

In the early 1920s, the Vincent brothers—Reasley, Lester, Jim, and George—established their fernery business, becoming part of the Zellwood Fern Growers Association. This group shipped its first ferns—approximately 285,000 of them—in the spring of 1923. The company's logo and motto were printed in color on Vincent Fernery envelopes between 1912 and 1923. Lester went on to establish his own business, Lester B. Vincent & Son Florist, in the early 1930s. (CVT.)

Lester B. Vincent & Son Florist (above) was a significant part of the Zellwood business community for more than eight decades, with most family members working there at some point. The flower shop was instrumental in planning and implementing community projects, especially the Central Florida Fair exhibits, which won many awards. Lester started his nursery in 1922, raising ferns and flowers. In 1939, he began a wholesale retail flower business. After Highway 441 was widened in 1958, the company opened a third building (below). In 1978, the Lester B. Vincent family purchased Apopka Florist, which is now operated by Bill Vincent, a third-generation member of the family. The family sold the Zellwood property in 1989; as of 2014, it housed the La Chaquita Mexican store. (Both, courtesy of Becky Vincent Juvinall.)

SCL DEPOT ZELLWOOD, FLA. 1970

ZELLWOOD FLA

The Zellwood Railroad Depot was located on the southwest corner of Jones Avenue and Highway 441. Leonard F. Stewart Sr. came to Zellwood as stationmaster for the Tavares, Orlando & Atlantic Railroad and served for 42 years. He joined a community bustling with activity. Stewart recalled hundreds of carloads of slate and tile being received to build the Sydonie mansion. A warranty deed from May 1885 (before the construction of Highway 441) shows that land was purchased by the Tavares, Orlando & Atlantic for a passenger depot where the old depot once stood and for a freight depot on the land where the Zellwood Fruit Distributors' packinghouse was located.

A group of unidentified friends went to the depot to bid adieu to young Estelle King (seated), who left Zellwood to attend Wesleyan College in Macon, Georgia. (JFB.)

The folks seen here in McHaffie's Grocery are, from left to right, Grace McHaffie, Fern Winn, Cal McHaffie (Grace's husband), Julia Fern Haynes, an unidentified woman, J.B. Haynes, Hazel Haynes, Elwood McHaffie, and Betty Ann Haynes. Buses brought fruit pickers to this store, where workers spent their pay. Cal passed away in 1968, leaving Grace to manage their orange groves and McHaffie's Grocery. (Courtesy of Jill Maltby Horton.)

Mae Borders (in white sweater) owned Borders Mercantile, north of Zellwood. Her daughter Sarah Tozia (in dark dress) and granddaughter Carol (in foreground, wearing skirt and socks) are also pictured. Borders purchased the mercantile in 1945 and demolished and rebuilt it in 1955, when Orange Blossom Trail was a four-lane road. Borders obtained laborers for other farmers and employed workers for her own farm. Del Monte contracted with Borders to grow Blue Lake beans. (Courtesy of Carol Adkins.)

27

Bateman's Cafe and General Store was located on Highway 441. There, one could board the Greyhound bus for all points north or south. For 50¢, one could ride all the way to Orlando to shop for clothing and shoes; the route was especially popular during the Christmas holidays. Teenagers without transportation could make a day of shopping and eating lunch at Morrison's Cafeteria. In the image below, Truma and Cliff Bateman pose in front of their business, Bateman's Café and General Store, with a group of unidentified children. Inell Miller recalls that the Batemans were wonderful people and were like parents to her when she rented from them. (Left, courtesy of Jill Maltby Horton; below, courtesy of Betty Smith Allen.)

Leonard F. Stewart Jr. (pictured at right) was born in Zellwood and served as postmaster from June 30, 1935, until January 1978. He cared about people and would often deliver important mail and packages to residents' homes, even on holidays. At 11:00 each evening, a huge bus called the "Mule Train" stopped behind the post office to deliver and pick up the mail. "Lenny," as he preferred to be called, also owned Stewart's Sundries drugstore and grew citrus. He was a veteran of World War II. (WL.)

Wallace Byron Osborn (pictured below) was appointed acting postmaster on August 4, 1928, following the death of his father, Lewis C. Osborn, who had served in the position since 1911. Wallace was later designated postmaster and served until 1935. At the time, the post office was a lean-to outside of Osborn General Merchandise on the east side of the intersection of Magnolia Street and Jones Avenue. A train left mail on an elevated hook on the railroad tracks beside the depot.

The Zellwood Post Office and Stewart's Sundries drugstore, owned by Leonard F. Stewart Jr., were constructed in 1946, before Highway 441 was widened to four lanes. Stewart was postmaster and managed the store with the help of his sister, Helen "Babe" Uptagraft. Through the years, he employed many Zellwood residents in the drugstore, including teenagers as young as 14. For some, the 50¢ hourly wage helped them purchase school clothes. Stewart, a friend to everyone, was devoted to his work and to the care of his mother, Annie. (Courtesy of Betty Uptagraft.)

Lois Miller Brown (left) and "Babe" Uptagraft (right) are pictured at Stewart's Sundries. The drugstore sold fountain drinks, coffee, soup, sandwiches, and Borden's Elsie ice cream for cones, sundaes, sodas, and milkshakes. People came to check the mail at the post office next door, then visited Stewart's. Customers included locals and out-of-towners. The Rock-Ola jukebox was a highlight for teenagers. Customers could also purchase various over-the-counter medicines and remedies, as well as perfumes and magazines. (Courtesy of Deloris Lynch.)

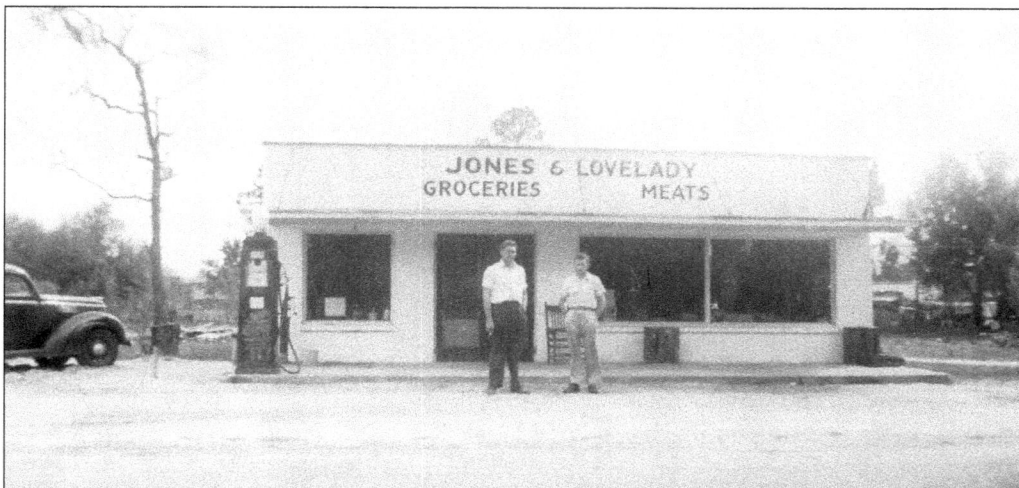

In 1930, Wallace Osborn sold the business that his brother Lewis once operated—Osborn General Merchandise—to William S. Jones. Jones and his wife, Florence, raised Evelyn Brawn after her father died. A few years later, the Joneses invited Brawn and her husband, W.D. Lovelady (at left in this image), to join the business. In 1946, the Jones & Lovelady store moved into this concrete building, which the store's owners had constructed at 5710 Jones Avenue. (WL.)

At 2651 North Orange Blossom Trail, on the northeast corner of Winifred Avenue and Highway 441, Ellis and Nadine Starbird built the Zellwood Truck Stop around 1956. "It was a full service truck stop with a nice lounge, bunks, showers, and Ellis's office," recalled Nadine. The Starbirds sold the truck stop in 1970. In 2014, Zellwood Country Kitchen was in this location and was typically packed with people enjoying breakfast and lunch. (Courtesy of Nadine Starbird.)

Marvel Walker (pictured at left with her husband, Walter) opened her first beauty shop in 1958 in her home beside the Zellwood Baptist Church. In 1960, the salon moved into a new building constructed on Highway 441 beside the Bay gas station. Many Zellwood residents were thrilled to have a beauty shop where women could go for a stylish haircut, permanent wave, or a new hair color. With mother's permission, teenagers could get blonde hair—just like the movie stars. (Courtesy of Marvel Walker.)

The road between Orlando and Zellwood was reportedly once a pine-needle path. The Florida Department of Transportation's earliest record for the main highway through Zellwood is dated 1920–1922. Though it was originally part of State Road 2, this highway was later renumbered State Road 500, and by 1936, it had been designated as Highway 441. In the 1940s, Highway 441 became a two-lane road. Around 1957, Zellwood storefronts lost property to the new four-lane highway, and stores also lost their curbside parking spaces. In this picture from the early 1960s, Inell Miller stands on the median of Highway 441. (Courtesy of Betty Smith Allen.)

Three

AGRICULTURE

Around 1922, Richard Whitney purchased the bankrupt Zellwood Farms Company along with its several thousand acres of muck land. It was renamed Zellwood Humus Company in 1925. The company mined peat, dried it, and sold it to gardeners and nurseries. In 1933, it began to make a profit, but in 1935, Whitney was accused of embezzlement; he admitted his guilt. The company tried to recover but was unsuccessful. (OC.)

The crop dusters shown here are Johnny Gardner (left), Robert Carroll Potter (center), and Francis "Red" Turner. Potter and Gardner owned the Airplane Dusting Service until the early 1960s, when that business ceased to exist. Potter stayed in the crop dusting business and operated Potter Flyers Incorporated at Zellwood until the State of Florida bought the farmland in the Zellwood Drainage District over a period of years in the late 1990s. (Courtesy of Jan Potter.)

This Stearman biplane was designed by Boeing Aircraft Company in the late 1930s to be used for training pilots in World War II. After the war, Stearmans were adapted for crop dusting. Robert Carroll Potter converted many biplanes into crop dusters, as shown in this image. The smokestack of the Zellwood Dehydration Plant is visible in the background. (Courtesy of Jan Potter.)

Bernard L. "Bob" Hughes is pictured above holding his son, Terry. Bob started crop dusting around Belle Glade in 1947 and, for a time, flew in both South Florida and Zellwood. In 1949, Bob moved to Zellwood. His father, Lawrence "Pop" Hughes (also a crop duster) soon followed. Bob and his brother Paul Edward Hughes leased McDonald airport, near Highway 441, from Marion McDonald and built a hangar. Paul piloted the Stearman pictured below. Elsewhere, west of Highway 441 on Jones Avenue, Pop established his own grass runway and built a house beside what was later called Bob White Field. In 1952, Bob Hughes was killed when his Stearman crop duster and Jerry Svrlinga's plane collided. Svrlinga was pulled from his plane by W.A. Keen. (Both, courtesy of the Hughes family.)

In this 1999 image, Jan Charles Potter, flying a Piper Brave PA-36-375, sprays sweet corn at Potter Farms in Zellwood. Spring corn was sprayed about 20 times to prevent armyworms from destroying the crop. Each fall, the corn required about 40 applications of pesticides. The Potters were Piper Aircraft dealers who helped Piper flight-test these airplanes. (Courtesy of Jan Potter.)

Emery Rice (left), Clare Roach (center), and Johnny Gardner pose with an alligator in this c. 1940 photograph. After crop dusters noticed the gator from the air, the sizeable reptile was removed to protect the safety of field workers. (Courtesy of Diana Rice Acree.)

Emery and Gladys Rice came to Zellwood from Indiana in 1945. The government sent Emery to Florida to run the Zellwood Dehydration Plant (visible in the background at right in the above image). After World War II ended, rations—such as dehydrated carrots and potatoes—were no longer necessary, so Emery, who had farmed from the start, raised corn to feed his cattle. Emery and Gladys's daughters, Ella Mae and Diana, are pictured above, and Emery and Gladys's son, Lynn, is pictured below on a tractor at the plant. (Both, courtesy of Diana Rice Acree.)

In the late 1940s, Perl Stutzman came from Ohio to Zellwood to farm; he devised the spray rig shown in the above image. Pictured below are Laura and Sanford Stutzman, Perl's parents, with a truckload of Zellwood corn. According to the July 4, 1948, edition of the *Orlando Morning Sentinel*, the Stutzmans received more for their corn per crate because it was of a higher quality; their 320 acres yielded $31,735 worth of corn sales in two days on the New York market. (Both, courtesy of Cletus Stutzman.)

In 1949, farmer Charles Grinnell Sr. photographed his 1929 Model A Ford carrying the morning's harvest of radishes picked by Ira Whatley (left), Cecil Jones (center), and J.C. Love (sitting on fender). Later in the day, the same crew washed the bunched radishes, packed them in wire-bound crates, and stacked them in a cold room to await transport to market. (CG.)

By 1981, Grinnell Farms' custom-made 10-row harvester could pick the equivalent of a 1949 half-truckload of radishes (shown in the previous image) in under 10 minutes. The harvester efficiently pulled radishes, cut off their leaves, and put them into wagons. Charles Grinnell Jr., pictured here on the harvester, assumed leadership at Grinnell Farms upon his father's retirement in 1984. (CG.)

In this 1960s photograph, Walter A. Duda inspects a leaf lettuce crop on the A. Duda & Sons, Inc., Zellwood farm. A third-generation member of the Andrew Duda family, Walter had an inherent love of farming and held a bachelor of science degree in agriculture from the University of Florida. In 1997, he was appointed president of Duda's farm division, which, by then, had operations in four states. He died in 1999 at age 63. (Courtesy of A. Duda & Sons, Inc.)

In 1946, the Duda brothers—John, Andrew, and Ferdinand—purchased several Tillavators (tilling machines manufactured in Wisconsin) that were well suited for the muck soils on their Zellwood farm. Along with their father, Andrew, the three brothers began their farming enterprise in Slavia, Florida, in 1926. The Zellwood farm provided a lengthened season for vegetable crops. This photograph was taken in the 1960s. (Courtesy of A. Duda & Sons, Inc.)

This 1980s image shows the A. Duda & Sons Zellwood farm from the air. The primary crops grown on the approximately 3,400-acre farm included carrots, celery, sweet corn, cabbage, and leaf items such as lettuce and parsley. Over its 50-plus-year history, the farm produced an estimated 80 to 100 million packages of vegetables. The farm began producing sod in 1980. (Courtesy of A. Duda & Sons, Inc.)

Dennis Robinson (left) began working on the A. Duda & Sons farm in 1948, retiring as its general manager in 1989. With him in this 1960s photograph is J.W. Fortson, who worked as a crop superintendent at the farm. Vernon "Buddy" Robinson (no relation to Dennis), who transferred to the Zellwood farm from the company's Belle Glade location in 1966, managed the farm until it was sold to the State of Florida in 1999. (Courtesy of A. Duda & Sons, Inc.)

41

Kenneth F. Jorgensen, a
Cornell University graduate
in agricultural economics,
worked for Beech-Nut
Packing Company in New
York. In 1944, Beech-Nut's
baby food and C-ration
business transferred Jorgensen
so that he could supervise its
new Zellwood farm. Plagued
by equipment shortages
(due to the war), hurricanes,
and insects, Beech-Nut sold
the farm to Jorgensen, Bob
Stewart, and Frank Dutton
in 1946; that year, the
men started Zellwin Farms
Company with 600 acres.
(Courtesy of Florida Fruit
and Vegetable Association.)

Kenneth Jorgensen's influence went beyond being dean of Zellwood's muck. From 1983 to 1985,
he was president of the Florida Fruit and Vegetable Association. He toured internationally
as agricultural advisor with Florida's then-secretary of agriculture, Doyle Connor. Jorgensen
(standing) died in 1998, as Zellwin Farms was transitioning after the state's buyout of the farm.
He was posthumously inducted into the Florida Agricultural Hall of Fame in 1999. (Courtesy of
Kathy Youngs.)

Zellwin Farms Company devoted the majority of its fields to growing carrots, corn, and radishes. It also grew escarole, chicory, romaine, Boston and Bibb lettuces, broccoli, cauliflower, watercress, beets, coriander, and several varieties of cabbage. Carrot harvesting machines (above) pulled carrots out of the ground and clipped the tops. Trucks took carrots to the packinghouse (below), where they were washed, sized, and graded before being automatically packed into 1-, 2-, 5-, or 50-pound bags. The carrots primarily went to the Eastern United States, though they were exported to Toronto and Montreal in winter months. Zellwin marketed its own produce and used independent truckers for delivery. (Both, courtesy of Glenn Rogers.)

Carrying on the famous Zellwood sweet corn tradition that started many years ago, the Scott family at Long & Scott Farms continues to grow the only "Zellwood Sweet Corn." They have updated their corn label, but the outstanding taste is still the same. In 1997, Long & Scott Farms built their first pole barn to house Scott's Country Market, which offered corn and a variety of seasonal produce. (Courtesy of Rebecca Scott Ryan.)

In 1957, Henry Swanson was an agricultural agent for Orange County. The county's yield ranked second in Florida and twenty-first in the United States. Swanson proposed using a photograph to illustrate that three acres of farmland would feed one person for a year. Billy Long obliged Swanson by plowing three acres of muck, stamping words into the muck with his boots, and filling the words with lime. Long is standing left of the "Y" to give perspective. (Courtesy of Billy Long.)

In 1963, Frank Scott (right), who had farmed in Virginia, joined Billy Long (left), a longtime friend, to create Long & Scott Farms. Long had started farming on the Zellwood muck in 1952. They combined efforts to clear the sandy land west of the muck, where Long & Scott Farms is today. This photograph was taken at Long & Scott Farms' 50th anniversary. (Courtesy of Billy Long.)

In 1965, Billy Long (far left) and his wife, Bobbie (second from left), flew to Fort Collins, Colorado, where Billy was named an Outstanding Young Farmer. The Jaycees sponsored the event, in which counties selected candidates. From those, each state submitted an entrant to compete at the national level. Billy Long's farming successes were recognized again when he was inducted into the Florida Agricultural Hall of Fame in 2005. (Courtesy of Billy Long.)

Around 1951, four Ohio farmers, including Franklyn Gaede (pictured), heard about the rich farmland in Zellwood. They bought 240 acres of muck land and leased 160 more acres. Their Ohio Farmers company owned 400 acres in Michigan, and the owners purchased trucks to haul the vegetables to Ohio, where they were packaged. At first, these farmers grew all kinds of vegetables. Later, crops were restricted to mainly radishes, along with some carrots and sweet corn. (Courtesy of Orlan and Connie Wichman.)

This image shows carrots being harvested under cloudy skies in the spring of 1998 at Stroup Farms, Inc. Dan Stroup began farming in Zellwood in 1957. Dan's son, Scott—and then Scott's son, Christopher (shown here pulling the wagon to collect the family's final carrot crop)—followed in his footsteps, carrying on the family farming tradition until 1998, when the Stroup farmland was bought by the State of Florida, as were most of the farms within the Zellwood Drainage District. Stroup Farms also grew corn, broccoli, and assorted greens. (Courtesy of Lillian Stroup.)

Farmers discovered numerous aboriginal dugouts on farms around Lake Apopka. In 1978, after plowing a radish field, the Grinnell family noticed chunks of charred wood. The Orlando Science Center sent Art Dreves (pictured) to investigate. He located a dugout estimated to be around 1,200 years old. Extremely heavy, waterlogged, and friable, it could not be moved without being destroyed. (Courtesy of the *Orlando Sentinel*.)

Mule trains were specially constructed for hand-harvesting and hand-packing sweet corn. The crates, which each held about 50 ears of corn, were assembled on top of the machine and then slid down chutes to the packing area. Pickers walked down the rows in front of the machine, placing ears in bins. Using this system, a crew could harvest 25 rows at a time. Once the corn was packed, the crates were stacked on a six-wheel flatbed truck. This truck was pulled through the field by the mule train, then unhooked when full (about 1,000 crates.) The corn was driven to a pre-cooler for hydro-cooling to about 36 degrees Fahrenheit. Refrigerated trucks delivered the corn all over the United States. (Courtesy of Jan Potter.)

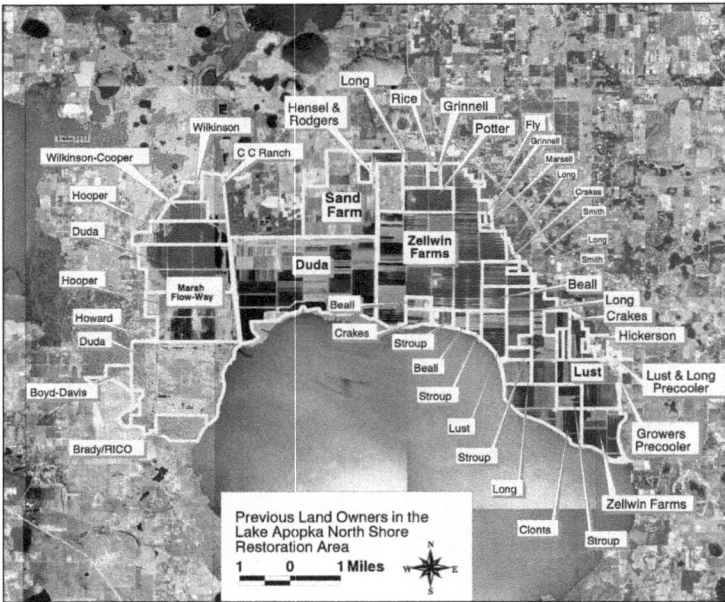

This map shows farms that were bought by the state in the late 1990s; the map also notes the previous landowners. The map shows Lake Apopka's North Shore Restoration Area (NSRA) within Orange and Lake Counties. The NSRA includes the land along the Zellwood side of Lake Apopka that had formerly been Duda farms, Zellwood Drainage District, and the Sand Farm. (Courtesy of James Peterson and St. Johns River Water Management District.)

In 1958, Ted Pope and Billy Long modeled Zellwood's Muck Suppers after Sanford farmers' Perishable Tramps. The so-called Zellwood Country Club, named by Tom Staley, served as the venue for the monthly suppers where farmers could socialize. This 1998 photograph shows the last meeting at the Zellwood Country Club. Sand Suppers at Long & Scott Farms carried on the tradition after the state's buyout of much of the land surrounding Lake Apopka. (Courtesy of Glenn Rogers.)

W.B. and Louise Shiver were Zellwood entrepreneurs from 1954 to 1981. The family homesteaded a strip between the railroad tracks and Highway 441, where they sold corn, tomatoes, and locally grown produce. Louise was a Cub Scout leader, and W.B. was the volunteer fire department commissioner. The couple is pictured at right; Louise is pictured below. (Both, courtesy of Deneth Shiver.)

The Sydonie dairy's herd of Jersey cows was under the care of head dairyman William White from Tennessee. The Sydonie dairy provided milk delivery to northwest Orange County until about 1925. According to Florida historian Jerrell H. Shofner, White bought T.J. King's dairy herd in 1926 and then sold milk directly to consumers.

Emery Rice stored dried corn in his granaries located south of Jones Avenue and half a mile west of Highway 441. In his airtight silos, Rice kept green fodder (silage or chopped corn stalks) used for feeding livestock in the winter. (Courtesy of Marion Rice.)

Originally from Scotland, William Edwards and his wife, Isobel, lived in the former T. Ellwood Zell home. Isobel organized Zellwood's first Girl Scout troop. William managed both Laughlin and Pirie Estates. He served as governor of Orlando General Hospital and as president of Florida Citrus Exchange, Plymouth Citrus Growers Association, Bank of Apopka, and the Orange County Chamber of Commerce. (Courtesy of Orange County Regional History Center.)

In this 1973 aerial photograph, the building for Lester B. Vincent and Son Florists is at far left. Directly behind the flower shop is the home of Lester and Clarice Vincent. The ranch-style home of Reasley Vincent Jr. and his wife, Dudley, is slightly above center. The 14 or so white edifices throughout are the greenhouses of Lester, Reasley Sr., and Reasley Jr. Ponkan Road is at the top of the image. Highway 441 slants from upper left to lower right, with railroad tracks running parallel to 441 along the bottom of the picture. Note the numerous orange groves, which were vital to the area's economy at the time. (Courtesy of Becky Vincent Juvinall.)

Ralph Meitin and Myer Shader founded Zellwood Fruit Distributors in 1943. The company employed approximately 130 people. This 1952 company photograph does not include truck

Plymouth Citrus Growers Association, affiliated with the Florida Citrus Exchange, was organized in 1910. The group rented a packinghouse on Highway 441 and purchased it in 1911. William Edwards, from Zellwood, served as president of the association for 20 years. He was succeeded

drivers or citrus pickers. The packinghouse, located by the railroad tracks near Highway 441 and Ponkan Road, burned down in March 1960. (Courtesy of Jon Miller.)

by E.W. Fly. The association employed many Zellwood residents. In the peak season, employees worked from early morning until 9:00 or 11:00 each night. The work was very laborious. (Courtesy of Deloris Lynch.)

Citrus was shipped under various labels from Zellwood Fruit Distributors. It went by railroad to the Northeast and Midwest and by truck to Atlanta and Columbia, South Carolina. "Fruit was the currency of Central Florida," wrote Isabel Wilkerson in *The Warmth of Other Suns*. (All images courtesy of Julian Meitin.)

These postcards show African Americans picking oranges. Pickers in Zellwood were employed by Libbey; Miller, Meitin, and Shader; Zellwood Fruit Distributors; Coen; Svrlinga Groves; and others. Pickers climbed 20- to 30-foot ladders with canvas bags strapped over their shoulders. The bags, which could hold 50 pounds of oranges, had a clip-style opening, allowing workers to empty the fruit from the bag into a box. Approximately 500 boxes, each holding 90 pounds of produce, could be harvested from an acre of orange trees. With one worker picking 10 boxes of oranges per hour, an acre would take 50 hours of harvest labor. As grove equipment evolved, pruning machines trimmed trees so that workers could pick from shorter ladders, and large, round bins replaced the wooden boxes. (Both, JFB.)

This float represented Dewkist, a trademark of Zellwood Fern Growers' Association, organized in 1922. The association shipped 285,000 ferns in the spring of the following year. During the 1925–1926 season, 850,000 ferns were shipped by this association, which marketed *Asparagus plumosus* and *Asparagus densiflorus* throughout the United States and parts of Canada. (Courtesy of Mary Wright.)

The azaleas outside of Reasley Vincent Jr.'s greenhouse exemplified the many beautiful flowers, plants, and ferns that he grew commercially. His father, Reasley Vincent Sr., was well known for his innovative propagation and development of new types and color combinations of violets and orchids. (Courtesy of Kathy Parker Rice.)

Jessie Hargroves (with a mule named Lightning) plows walkways between ferns at Marsell's Fernery. Anne and Elmer Marsell started their business in 1924, growing ferns on Round Lake Road. Their leatherleaf ferns were grown under slat sheds. At peak times, 50 to 60 workers cut ferns. Cutters were wary of snakes, and in 1956, a black panther was said to frequent the sheds at night. (Courtesy of Laurie Marsell.)

Allen Sewell stands in one of the first glass greenhouses in Zellwood. E.W. Fly bought and shipped the glass from the north. Sewell served as the foreman at Fernwood Nursery for over 15 years. During that time, Fernwood grew philodendron and sansevieria plants. It was hot and humid in the greenhouses—uncomfortable for workers, but exactly what the plants needed to thrive. (Courtesy of Louise Roberts.)

A group of Fernwood workers poses in the above 1940s photograph. E.W. "Walter" Fly started Fernwood Nursery in the 1930s at the end of Wesley Road. Originally, the nursery grew Boston ferns outdoors under oaks. Later, the company made sheds with two-by-four posts holding up slats; spacers let sunlight through. The nursery shipped cut ferns to florists. Workers lit smudge pots, spaced about 30 feet apart, to protect ferns during extremely cold weather. Boilers later replaced the smudge pots; propane gas heaters followed. Plastic sheets kept the heat in the sheds. Walter's son, Edwin Fly, graduated from the University of Florida, served in World War II, and then worked at Fernwood. In the early 1960s, the women shown below were among those who worked at Fernwood. They are, from left to right, Betty Smith, Lorene Brown, Lula Martin, unidentified, and Gladys Martin. (Above, courtesy of Sue Hazelwood; below, courtesy of Betty Smith Allen.)

Four

MILITARY

This honor roll of Zellwood's citizens in military service during World War II was located on Jones Avenue east of Leon and Violet Osborn's home. Servicemen met the bus to leave for duty on Highway 441. An Army camp was located in a field on Lake Maggiore not far from this sign. Several blocks away, soldiers took in plays and music at Zellwood Elementary School. (WL.)

Lafayette "Fate" Humphrey was 18 when he volunteered for the Army during World War I. He was wounded in battle by poison gas. While recovering in France, he learned how to be an excellent cook. Humphrey brought home exciting stories. He told about hundreds of warhorses being put to death rather than being transported home and how their bones are in the soil of France's great flower-growing area near Marseille. (Courtesy of Jack Humphrey.)

Cpl. James Arlington Vincent (right) was sent overseas along with thousands of other doughboys in cattle ships to win "the war to end all wars." Vincent served in France, Luxembourg, and Belgium from July 16, 1918, to July 31, 1919. Vincent's hair turned white and he lost his hearing during the war. He came home to Zellwood, married Gladys Margaret Cooper, and, together, they raised four children. (CVT.)

This Civil Air Patrol tower was erected in 1942 in a field where Lake Maggiore Estates is currently located. After the bombing of Pearl Harbor, the government established a Civil Defense Program in every community and county to protect the coastal United States. The towers were manned 24 hours a day by volunteers searching the skies for enemy aircraft. (OC.)

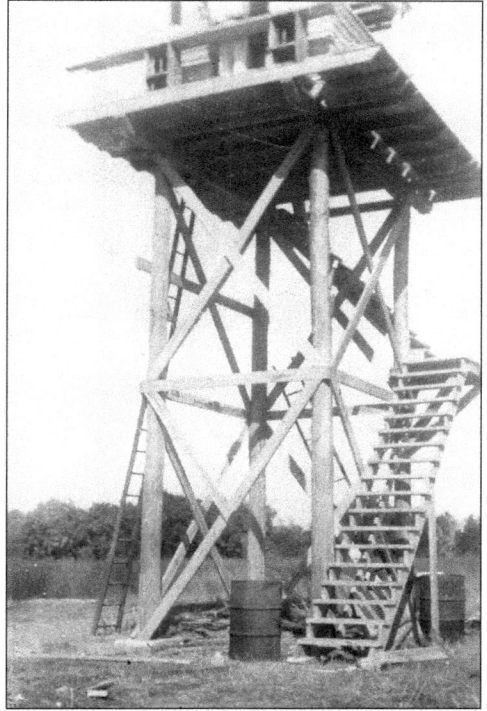

World War II servicemen and their mothers are documented in this c. 1945 photograph. Pictured here are, from left to right, Marion Sheddan and his mother, Louise Sheddan; George A. Vincent and Annie Vincent; J.H. Brown with Lily Ethel Brown; Bob Morton, Lou Morton (mother of Bob and Paul), and Paul Morton; and Edwin Fly, Leila Fly (mother of Edwin and Wesley), and Wesley Fly. (Courtesy of Honey Caldwell.)

Dwight Doggett was 18 when he enlisted in the Army in 1944. He served overseas with the 1748 Engineer Petroleum Group. Next, Doggett was part of the Ryukus campaign on Ie Shima and Okinawa. Finally, he was sent to Korea as part of the Army of Liberation. In 1992, as a civilian Doggett originated Zellwood's annual Memorial Day service at Conquest Cemetery. (Courtesy of Dwight Doggett.)

Tom Staley's Navy tour of duty aboard the USS Stern took him from European ports to Pearl Harbor. He experienced the esprit de corps when the flag was planted atop Mount Suribachi on Iwo Jima. After his discharge, Staley served as production manager at Zellwin Farms, where he interacted with German farm laborers who had been transported from a Leesburg POW camp to hoe and harvest. (Courtesy of Tom Staley.)

Zellwood-born Reasley Vincent Jr. flew B-17s and B-29s during World War II. Called back to serve in Korea, he flew KC-97s (refuelers to the B-47). Vincent originally joined the Army Air Corps, which later became the Air Force. After his service, Vincent went into the nursery business and attended On-the-Job Veterans' Training at Ocoee. (Courtesy of Mary Wright.)

While serving in the engineer corps of Patton's Third Army, Capt. Charles Grinnell Sr. helped build bridges for US troops moving across Europe. Grinnell received a Seaboard Air Line Railway pamphlet promoting Zellwood's muck farms. He saved much of his Army pay with the intention of beginning his own farm (Grinnell Farms), which he did after leaving the service in 1945. (CG.)

NCK LAND DRAINED, PLOWED AND HARROWED

Heavy Machinery
May Be Utilized

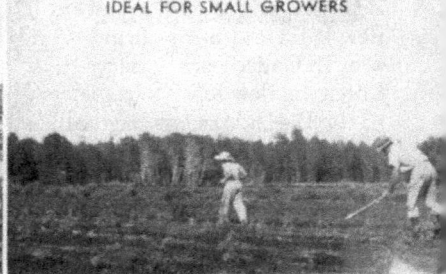
IDEAL FOR SMALL GROWERS

CUT-OVER LANDS ADJACENT TO THE MUCK
SOILS ARE SPLENDIDLY ADAPTED FOR LIVE STOCK

PREPARING ZELLWOOD MUCK FOR PLANTING

ZELLWOOD
FLORIDA

CANALS FOR DRAINAGE AND IRRIGATION

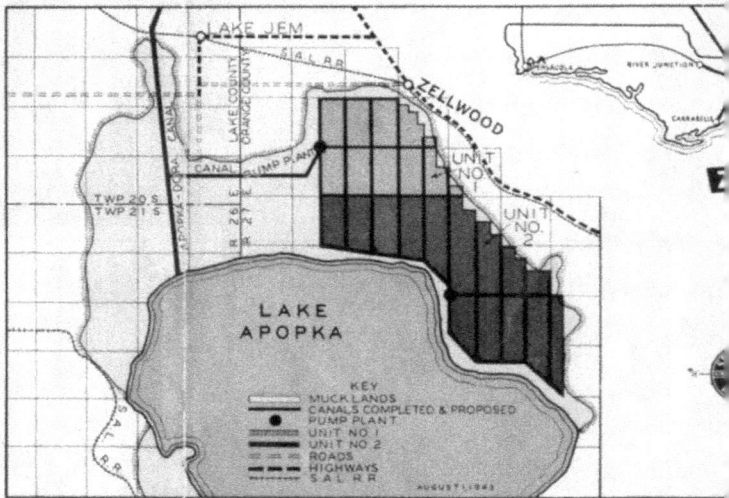

LAKE JEM

LAKE COUNTY
ORANGE COUNTY

ZELLWOOD

CANAL

CANAL PUMP PLANT

TWP 20 S
TWP 21 S

R 26 E R 27 E

UNIT NO 1

UNIT NO 2

E

LAKE
APOPKA

S.A.L.
R.R.

KEY
MUCK LANDS
CANALS COMPLETED & PROPOSED
PUMP PLANT
UNIT NO 1
UNIT NO 2
ROADS
HIGHWAYS
S.A.L.R.R.

AUGUST 1,1943

GOOD FISHING IN LAKES AND CANALS

HOLLY ARMS HOTEL, ZELLWOOD

SEABOARD
AIR LINE
RAILWAY
THROUGH THE HEART OF THE SOUTH

ZELLWOOD AREA IS WELL ADAPTED TO CITRUS FRUITS

GOOD HIGHWAYS

64

SPRING CELERY

GOOD FARM ROADS PERMIT USE OF HEAVY HAULING EQUIPMENT

Plant — Zellwood Drainage District

IRISH POTATOES DO EXCEEDINGLY WELL

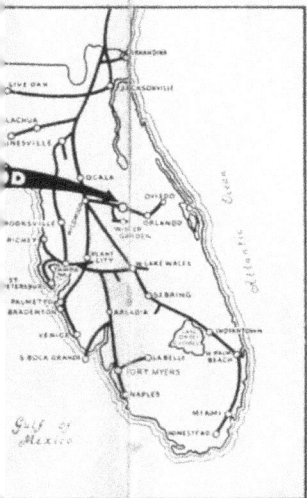

FAST FREIGHT SERVICE VIA SEABOARD AIR LINE

PACKING HOUSES FOR VEGETABLE CROPS ARE AVAILABLE

GOOD HOME

DEHYDRATING, CANNING AND OTHER PROCESSING PLANTS ARE BEING ESTABLISHED

This brochure, published by Seaboard Air Line Railway, was designed to promote farming in Zellwood, thereby increasing business for the railroad. After his discharge from the Army, Charles Grinnell rode the bus from New Jersey to Zellwood and began six decades of farming on the muck land. The pamphlet's foldout mentioned the Zellwood Drainage District and depicted rich land promising harvests of vegetables that could be dehydrated, canned, processed, or sold fresh. The Seaboard Air Line Railway promised to transport produce to market in good condition. (CG.)

65

In the Air Force, Robert "Carroll" Potter trained cadets and, later, flight instructors. After being transferred to Military Air Transport Command, Potter delivered B-24, B-25, C-46, and C-47 planes. Later, he flew missions across the Himalayan Mountains. After the war, Potter was a FAA flight examiner in Central Florida. In Zellwood, he started Potter Flyers, Inc. (a crop-dusting business) and Potter Farms. Potter logged over 35,000 hours in his flight book. (Courtesy of Jan Potter.)

Wilber Sewell joined the US Navy in September 1951 and traveled to San Diego for basic training. He received orders to board the DD-644 destroyer USS *Stembel*. The ship deployed to Korean waters and joined Task Force 77, consisting of two aircraft carriers, two cruisers, one battle ship, and eighteen destroyers. Sewell deployed four times to Korea during his tenure in the Navy. Upon returning to Zellwood, he worked in Ralph Lister's machine shop. (Courtesy of Wilber Sewell.)

Sgt. Edward Brown entered the US Army on August 19, 1940, at Fort Benning, Georgia. He was in the Third Army 802 Field Artillery. On July 4, 1944, Brown left Camp Shanks, New York, and he arrived in Scotland on July 16, 1944. Sergeant Brown served in Patton's 3rd Army in the Battle of the Bulge in Germany. He was also in combat in Belgium, Rhineland, and France. Discharged in 1945, he moved to Zellwood and worked for Fly's Humus Company and A. Duda and Sons. (Courtesy of Deloris Brown Lynch.)

Ronald Edward Brown (son of Sgt. Edward Brown) enlisted in the Marine Corps on August 28, 1963. Sergeant Brown served in the Vietnam War in ChuLai, Phubai, Donhai, and the DMZ from May 1965 until June 1966. Brown was in the Fire Direction Center of the 3rd Battalion, 12th Marines H Battery. He served as president of the Vietnam Veterans in Ocala and currently owns South Eastern Counseling Center in Winter Park. (Courtesy of Ron Brown.)

William Davis "W.D." Lovelady was an aircraft mechanic in the Army Air Corps during World War II. After initial training at Camp Blanding, near Starke, Florida, and aviation maintenance school, he served in England with the US 8th Air Force, repairing and maintaining P-51 Mustang fighter planes. (WL.)

William R. Lovelady Jr. (left), grandson of William Davis "W.D." Lovelady, poses with Iraqi army colonel Abbas Fadhil Abdul-Sahib at the Besmaya Range Complex in Iraq. Lovelady was a Navy reservist when he was mobilized to work in the public affairs office of the Multi-National Security Transition Command–Iraq in Baghdad. Abbas, who was the first officer to join the new Iraqi Army, presented the Iraqi flag to Lovelady as a gift during his visit to the range. (WL.)

In 1964, at 21 years of age, Zellwood-born Eugene Mason joined the Army; he served for 22 years. His Army tours of duty included Korea; Alaska; Germany; Fort Bliss, Texas; Fort Riley, Kansas; and Japan. Mason served as a cook, career counselor, and food service sergeant. (Courtesy of Eugene Mason.)

Lynn Rice married Marion Ellis, his high school sweetheart. The couple had a three-month-old son, Randy, when Lynn was drafted into the Army in July 1954. During the Korean War, Rice headed a motor pool unit that worked to protect New York City. After leaving the service, Rice returned to Zellwood and became a nurseryman. The Rice children and grandchildren continued to work in the nursery industry. (Courtesy of Marion Rice.)

Jimmy Willis served in the Army between 1969 and 1971. He underwent basic training at Fort Benning, Georgia, and advanced infantry training at Fort Polk, Louisiana. Jimmy married Janice Fountain (both of them are pictured here) 17 days before he went to Vietnam with the 1st Cavalry Division. Willis returned to Zellwood after being honorably discharged, and he wrote poems and a song dedicated to the memory of a fellow soldier; he performed the song at the Zellwood Historical Society's annual open houses in 2013 and 2014. (Courtesy of Jimmy Willis.)

Gene Sikes left Zellwood early in 1965 after joining the Army. He married in mid-1965, and his wife, Margaret, went with him to Fort Gordon, Georgia, and Sandia Base, New Mexico. After serving for a year in Vietnam, he became a military police self-defense instructor at Fort Gordon, where his daughter Deanie was born. Gene Sikes now lives in Zellwood and is the service/special projects district manager for Harper Limbach. (Courtesy of Gene Sikes.)

Five

ESTATES AND HOME LIFE

In this c. 1911 photograph, Jones Vincent (1848–1931) rests in a vintage lounge chair in front of The Old Nest, a home built by his son Reasley Vincent Sr. Jones and his first wife, Sophronia, had four children: Lou (Morton), Fredonia (Pugh), May (Vines), and William. After Sophronia died, Jones married Eliza and had seven more children: Reasley Wesley; Cicily (Gregory); Clifford (Wicker); George; Banella; Lester Brittian, and James Arlington Vincent. (CVT.)

Beginning in the 1920s, the Vincent, Morton, and Pugh families held many reunions at the first home of Lester and Clarice Vincent, which was located in Merrimac, between Zellwood and Plymouth. The family enjoyed frequent get-togethers, with great cooks providing a multitude of delicious dishes. They danced to the music of Banella Vincent playing piano, Lester Vincent strumming the mandolin, and James A. Vincent on the drums. (Courtesy of the Vincent family.)

Geraldine Shollenberg (left), along with Brittian (center) and Agnes Vincent, celebrate the end of school in May 1924 in front of The Old Nest. Stamped on the back of the photograph is the following: "Finished By B.G. Porter Eustis, Fla." Porter Photo, started in 1909, served the Eustis area for four generations starting. (Courtesy of Kathy Parker Rice.)

Reasley Vincent Sr. and his wife, Annie Allen Vincent, lived beneath shady oaks west of Donald Street in this two-story house built by Tom Morton and facing Highway 441. The Vincents' children, Reasley Jr., George A., and Hortense, were born here. The family raised chickens and cows and planted corn. Later, Annie's parents—A.C. Allen and his wife, Hortense—moved in with the Vincents. (Courtesy of the Orange County Regional History Center.)

This Florida Cracker home with a wraparound porch was located behind the railroad depot. Three generations lived in this house—Leonard F. Stewart Sr. and his wife, Annie; Leonard Jr. ("Lenny"); and Helen "Babe" Uptagraft and her son, George. Leonard Sr. served as stationmaster for the railroad for 42 years and as Zellwood Community Council president. Lenny was postmaster and owner of Stewart's Sundries. Babe worked in the post office and Stewart's Sundries. The family was known for being friends to all, hardworking, and accommodating to the citizens of Zellwood. (Courtesy of Betty Uptagraft.)

This surviving Classical Revival home, known as Odenwald, was built by W. Oden Hughart in 1879. Hughart was born in Kentucky, practiced law in Baltimore, and later became manager of the first telegraph line at Baltimore, Morse & Kendall. While he was president of the Grand Rapids & Indiana Railway, Hughart would park his private railcar on a sidetrack while he visited his cronies, spending winters in Zellwood. (CG.)

On the heels of Thomas Ellwood Zell and settlers drawn to Zellwood came Pittsburgh steel magnate James Laughlin Jr. and his wife, Sidney Page Laughlin. In 1895, construction of Laughlin's winter home (pictured below) was overseen by Edgar V. Seeler, who also selected the furnishings. By 1904, the Arts and Crafts mansion with Mediterranean Revival touches was completed. An iron gate complemented the arch facing Odenwald, which was situated to the east.

The Laughlins' carriage house was covered with vines and had lanterns on posts and a pit for mechanics. East of the carriage house was the estate's powerhouse. In the heyday of Laughlin Estate (1886–1919), its annual operating expense was $80,000. William Edwards managed the estate with mechanics, carpenters, and 49 full-time gardeners. In the 1930s, Pierre Wilds DuBose bought the estate to house Hampden DuBose Academy. These buildings became classrooms.

A Laughlin Estate guest who gazed across Lakes Minore and Maggiore from the covered porch of the grandest home, Sydonie (named for James Laughlin Jr.'s wife, Sidney Page Laughlin) might have noticed the sparkling stucco surface of the building and incorrectly supposed that it was constructed of concrete. Sydonie was built of yellow pine and lined with a thin layer of slate. Stucco was applied over the exterior.

John Wesley King married Sue Cross in 1881. Their children were Edwin F. King, Arthur R. King, Leila Clyde King, and Estelle King. A nephew, Fain English, was raised as King's own son. Sue died on February 24, 1918. He was later remarried to Marian Haynes of Leesburg, Florida. This family gathering includes, from left to right, (first row) Wesley Fly, Estelle King, Arthur King, Fain English King; (second row) Edwin King, Erastus W. "Walter" Fly, John Wesley King, Edwin Fly, Jolene King (holding unidentified baby), Leila Clyde King Fly, and an unidentified woman. (JFB.)

The two-and-a-half-story King house (pictured) was built in the Fleming Addition in 1911, when John Wesley and Sue King moved to Zellwood from Mount Pleasant, Tennessee. This high-style Queen Anne home at 5151 King Avenue had gas lighting. Panel doors could be pulled together to conceal the octagonal living room from the foyer. King dealt in citrus and general merchandise. (JFB.)

76

Erastus "Walter" Fly came from Mount Pleasant, Tennessee, in 1911 and married Leila Clyde King after courting via mail and infrequent visits. At right, Walter holds their young son, Edwin Walter, as firstborn John Wesley stands with Leila. The family's residence (below) was at 3368 Washington Street. In the 1920s, Leila was treasurer for Zellwood's Community Council. After first serving as an educator, Walter Fly was active in ferneries, citrus, and real estate. He established Fernwood Nurseries and co-owned Fly and Lyon Real Estate. Walter served in various official capacities for Plymouth Growers' Association, Zellwood Fern Growers, Apopka State Bank, and Zellwood Methodist Church. (Right, JFB; below, courtesy of the Orange County Regional History Center.)

Julia McDonald's former home, reportedly constructed around 1884, still stands at 5402 King Street. It was refurbished a few years ago. Located two houses east of the wooden Zellwood Elementary School (which has since burned down), it was a convenient place for a few of Zellwood's early teachers and principals to room and board. This tin-roofed, hard pine, board-and-batten Cracker home had a carriage house toward the back with a covered parking place for a buggy, an area for horses to eat hay, and a small hayloft. (Courtesy of Deloris Lynch.)

In 1910, John and Lou Morton built a two-story house on King Road with an orange grove, a slatted fern house, and a vegetable garden. Of the family's six children, Dorothy and Robert ("Bob") were born in Zellwood. Bob became a World War II veteran, an officer for Zellwood Water Users and Zellwood Drainage District, superintendent of Sunday school at Zellwood Methodist, and comptroller of Fernwood Nursery. Byron Morton McCoy, daughter of John and Lou, tended the garden and hosted quilting parties at the home until her death in 1990. (Courtesy of Deloris Lynch.)

This stately home, owned by Violet and Leon Osborn, was located on the corner of Highway 441 and Jones Avenue. The lovely sunporch was filled with vintage wicker furniture. The Stewart sisters, Helen ("Babe") and Margaret, were married in a double wedding here. Anne Self (Langford), a schoolteacher in 1907, stayed at the Osborn home; she was the mother of Carl Langford, who later served as mayor of Orlando. (OC.)

Leon and Violet Osborn met in Orlando while he was teaching science at Orlando High School. The couple, married for 42 years, lived in the beautiful old Victorian Osborn homestead on Jones Avenue. Violet taught for one year at Zellwood Elementary and then at Delaney Elementary for five years. The Osborns' contributions to early Zellwood are too numerous to name. She was devoted to the Zellwood Library and kept it open for a long period of time. Leon recorded the history of Zellwood in his writings. The following is an excerpt from Leon's notebook: "Zellwood even from its beginning has been a village aspiring to the better things in life. In the early days calling cards, gloves and appointments for the ladies were in vogue. There were plays, debates and elaborate parties." (OC.)

William "W.D." Lovelady and Evelyn Brawn married in Zellwood in 1939. W.D., friends, and family built the couple's wood frame home (left) at 5444 Jones Avenue. It was completed during the couple's honeymoon. In the kitchen, shown below with corner cupboard and ruffled curtains, Evelyn made meals for her husband and their son, Bill. She prepared the fish they caught or the quail they shot. Evelyn hosted parties, inviting neighborhood children for birthdays, Christmas, Halloween, and get-togethers after Methodist Youth Fellowship meetings. The Loveladys were known by practically everyone in Zellwood because they owned and operated the Jones and Lovelady store—a social hub of the community. (Both, WL.)

Gladys Cooper Vincent is proudly displaying a bass that she baked whole and served with an olive sauce, a family favorite. Gladys and her husband, Jim, built their downtown Zellwood home in the mid-1920s with pine trees they cut themselves. They hauled them by horse and cart to the Rock Springs sawmill, which produced their heart-pine floors. Jim retired from Plymouth Citrus Growers, spent his days fishing, and kidded that he had the fishing disease, joking, "Thank God, there's no cure!" Gladys retired after driving the local school bus for 37 years—a state record. She was known for her homemade pies; she once made seven or more a day for their barbecue stand. (CVT.)

In the Vincent home, the family's first three children—Marguerite Bernice, James Gleason, and Donald Cooper— were born with the aid of midwives. Their fourth child, Cicily, was born in Waterman Memorial Hospital in Eustis. All of Gladys and Jim Vincent's children enjoyed their childhood in Zellwood, with Marguerite declaring it "a wonderful place to grow up!" The picture at left shows Marguerite at age three and James at age one. (CVT.)

In the 1940s and 1950s, Army barracks were brought into town and sold or rented to families moving to Zellwood. They were long enough for two families to share by partitioning off the middle. Many families who rented former barracks had come from Georgia to work in the citrus industry. Wanting better living conditions, they purchased lots and started building little frame houses. Allen Sewell was sought after to help construct homes similar to the one in the below photograph. With Sewell's carpentry skills and the help of relatives, one house after another was completed. Most of these homes, with the exception of Joe and Mattie Williford's, were constructed on a dirt road that Sewell called Silk Stocking Avenue (it was later named McDonald Street). In the 1950s, several families bought houses built by the Jim Walter Homes Company. The Shivers, Batemans, Sikes, and Browns moved into these homes, which featured a picture window in the living room. The home of Earl, Josephine, Ann, and "Skeet" White, pictured above, was located down a dirt road called Beck Street. (Above, courtesy of "Skeet" White; below, courtesy of Louise Roberts.)

As a teenager, Clarence F. Whitney hitchhiked from his native Vermont to the Carolinas. He graduated from Chapel Hill College of Education, then taught school in Zellwood and Apopka—thus his nickname, "Prof." He and his wife, Bess, lived on Union Street in a house that Prof continually added on to over the years. The Whitney house is visible in the background of this image. Vernon Maltby (pictured, holding fish) and his family lived in the house in the foreground. (Courtesy of Jill Horton.)

In the 1940s, eight (out of eleven) siblings from the Miller family moved to Zellwood from Georgia. Pictured here are some sisters and cousins from this huge family. They gathered weekly at different homes to enjoy delicious Southern cooking. The children took turns churning homemade ice cream, but they were forbidden to go out on the lake in the old rowboat at Steve (the oldest of the Miller siblings) and Henrietta Miller's home—they did so anyway. (Courtesy of Deloris Lynch.)

This white and brown frame vernacular house at 3213 Union Street was home to Lily Ethel Brown. Her canned goods were displayed annually at the Central Florida Fair, where she won blue ribbons and cash for the Zellwood Community Center. When Brown brought a roaster pan piled with her fried bread to a community dinner, there was never any left. (CG.)

A number of houses were transported to Zellwood from the Wilson Cypress lumber camp near Cassia, Florida. The house shown here fits the profile of a Wilson Cypress camp house. Unable to sustain business due to gasoline rationing during World War II, Wilson Cypress shut down its Cassia camp in 1942, and the wood frame houses once used for camp workers were sold at rock-bottom prices. Mr. Bowers of Apopka moved these structures. (Courtesy of Eugene Mason.)

Six

CHURCHES

Mr. and Mrs. Richard G. Robinson donated five acres for the site of the St. James Episcopal Mission Church on the north side of Church Street (present-day King Street). Mrs. John A. Williamson (Thomas Ellwood Zell's sister-in-law) and Mrs. Robinson established this church in 1878. This photograph shows the church's interior in 1914, when it was decorated for the marriage of Leila Clyde King and Erastus "Walter" Fly. When the original oil-burning chandeliers (which had to be pulled down to be lit) were aglow, they illuminated the stained-glass windows. This building no longer exists. (JFB.)

Richard Robinson guided construction of the first St. James Episcopal Mission Church. The town's men worked on Saturdays, splitting the timbers for the church by hand. A storm wrecked the first building in 1880. Services were held in a small log schoolhouse until a Gothic-style replacement (pictured) was built in 1885. After the mission closed in the 1930s, its bell was installed at Zellwood Methodist Church, where its ringing still signals the start of services each Sunday. Some of St. James's interior furnishings went to the Church of the Holy Spirit in Apopka, Florida, in the early 1940s. (JFB.)

Several families in Zellwood's Slovak community became members of St. Luke's Lutheran Church, founded in 1912 in Slavia Colony near Oviedo. This July 20, 1924, photograph of children being confirmed includes seven Zellwood children (from the Potsko, Ondich, and Svrlinga families). Pictured here are, from left to right, (first row) Adam Packo (Potsko), Katherine Mikler, Mary Ondich, Mary Lukas, Mary Mikler, Bessie Svrlinga, and Anthony Ondich; (second row) Pastor L.A. Jarosi, John Packo (Potsko), Joe B. Mikler, Andrew Ondich, Joseph Ondich, Joe L. Mikler, and Vicar John Bajus. (Courtesy of the Archives of St. Luke's Lutheran Church.)

Zellwood's Church of God started with 14 members in 1924, following revivals they held in the Episcopal church and Zellwood school. Early members recalled a sawdust floor, a hand-powered water pump, and a hen nesting in the building. The Happy Goodmans and Love Brothers vocal groups came from this church, which was noted for its music. The congregation is pictured here around 1947 in front of the church's building at 5221 King Avenue. (Courtesy of Dan Combs.)

The congregation from the First Baptist Church of Zellwood met in Levi Holloway's home on Highway 441 before it was formally chartered in 1946. Marvel Walker was among the charter members. In 1947, the church building on Winifred Street was completed with wooden benches and a dirt floor. On February 6, 1957, it was designated First Baptist Church of Zellwood. With an infusion of money, it evolved into a modern place to worship. (Courtesy of First Baptist Church of Zellwood.)

In 1906, Zellwood Methodist Church began with a gathering in Lewis Osborn's home. The congregation formally organized in 1911 with 12 charter members. Practically everyone in Zellwood helped build the sanctuary, which was completed in 1925. With a membership of 50, the first service was held in October 1925. Zellwood United Methodist Church celebrated its 100th anniversary in 2011. (JFB.)

In this photograph from the late 1920s, Annice Wenger (far left) stands beside her father, Thomas McGraw, first tenor in the Zellwood Quartet. Completing the group are, from left to right, Lester Bill Vincent, second tenor; Tom Morton Sr., second bass; and Claude Bell, first bass. Zellwood Methodist Church was their home, but the group was invited to sing in Orlando, Ocoee, and many other locations. Annice's mother, Ruth McGraw, was their pianist until her death in 1935. Evelyn Brawn then became the group's pianist. Today, the names of Annice Wenger and Tom McGraw appear under a stained-glass window along the west wall of Zellwood United Methodist Church. (Courtesy of Annice Wenger.)

Lake Ola Chapel was started on June 1, 1958, and supported by the Mount Dora Baptist Church. The mission was nicknamed "The Bird House" after the previous owner's last name, Parakeet. The building (above) was located just south of the Lake Ola Beach Motel facing Highway 441. The chapel's motto was "A friendly service with a vital message of the living Christ." In February 1962, Lake Ola Chapel relocated and broke ground at its current site on the corner of Highway 441 and Sadler Road. The church was constituted as Lake Ola Baptist Church in October 1964 (below). The congregation continued to build as it grew, and the current building was dedicated on March 12, 1967. In 2011, the church's name was changed to First Baptist Church of Tangerine. (Courtesy of First Baptist Church of Tangerine.)

In 1977, a billboard by the orange grove between Junction Road and Zellwood Station's entrance announced Rolling Hills Community Church. George Johnson donated land for the church site. While the new building was being designed and constructed, Rev. Harold DeRoo began holding organizational services at Zellwood Elementary School on August 21, 1977. The congregation visited Zellwood United Methodist Church and later rented a Seventh-Day Adventist building for Sunday services. Rev. Robert Schuller (second from right, with Reverend DeRoo) came from California to speak during the dedication of the new building on March 19, 1980. (Courtesy of Rolling Hills Community Church.)

The first regular church service at 4407 North Orange Blossom Trail (pictured) was held on March 23, 1980. Rolling Hills Community Church is part of the Reformed Church in America. (Courtesy of Rolling Hills Community Church.)

The Open Door Church of God in Christ began as a tent church. It was founded in 1949 by the first pastor, Maryetta Williams. The tent was replaced with a concrete building constructed at 3512 Marsell Road on land donated by Arthur Williams. Minnie L. Johnson is currently the pastor of the Open Door Church of God in Christ. (Courtesy of Eugene Mason.)

When Pauline Williams came to Zellwood in 1935, she missed the African Methodist Episcopal (AME) church, so she started the Mt. Zion AME Church on her porch. As the congregation grew, it needed a building, and the church purchased a quarter-acre of land and a two-room structure for $50. The cornerstone of today's Mt. Zion AME church (pictured) was laid on September 6, 1998. The church survived storms, fires, and a deceitful business deal. (Courtesy of Eugene Mason.)

Mayetta Sexton (left) started several churches before her death in 2009. She built a church on Holly Street, which burned down. The Fish House and Silver Slipper bars became churches with her influence. In the 1970s, Sexton bought the old wooden Zellwood Elementary School cafeteria and had it moved to Willow Street to become The Independent House of Prayer (above). (Above, courtesy of Hannah Brown Bloser; left, courtesy of Gwendolyn Dawson.)

In 1960, these Zellwood women were known as the Praying Warriors. They are, from left to right, Ola Bush, Pearl Mason (Ola Bush's daughter), Rosa Lee Williams, Evelyn Dunn, Annie Lee Smith, unidentified, Nellie Holden, Martha Bell, Mayetta Sexton, Berdie Mae Tarver, and Josephine Pollock. The child is Reginald Reddick. (Courtesy of Pearl Mason.)

Originally designated on the deed as "Tangerine Colored Cemetery," this site is now called Tangerine Cemetery. It was established in 1896, when the property was owned by Dudley and Hannah Adams of Tangerine. This is the headstone of Ruth Jackson, who died in 1897 and was one of the first people laid to rest in the cemetery. A committee of local citizens has maintained the older section, and plots are available in the newer section. (Courtesy of Hannah Brown Bloser.)

Evergreen Cemetery, established in 1890, is just north of Zellwood on Cemetery Road. The graves hold veterans from the Battle of Gettysburg, the Confederate army, World War I, World War II, and the Vietnam War. There are also Bronze Medal winners interred at Evergreen. In 1966, the Zellwood Garden Club improved the site. Evergreen was the final resting place for most Zellwoodians until the rediscovery of Conquest Cemetery in 1975. (Courtesy of Max Horton.)

Around 1880, J.D. Wilkins donated Conquest Cemetery to the Conquest Methodist Church. The earliest burial was Mary A. Goolsby (1821–1880). The site included the hanging tree and a section containing unmarked graves of slaves. The cemetery was rediscovered in 1975 during the development of Zellwood Station, and Zellwood United Methodist Church assumed responsibility for the site. In 1994, this entryway was dedicated to the memory of Gladys and James A. Vincent, longtime Zellwood residents. (Courtesy of Max Horton.)

Seven

COMMUNITY ACTIVITIES

This is the group photograph taken at the 1938 Fourth of July picnic in Zellwood. The 1930 annual Fourth of July community picnic was delayed due to illness. On July 23, at 3:00 a.m., Reasley, James, and Gladys Vincent started cooking 103 pounds of pork. By 10:00 that morning, Zellwood's citizens had converged at Rock Springs for contests on land and in the cold springwater. Appetites piqued, and the barbeque started at 1:00 p.m. (Courtesy of Laurie Marsell.)

Zellwood's baseball squad, The Mudhens, played on a field off of Robinson Street. Fans perched on wooden bleachers under an oak tree. This 1940s photograph appeared in the *Orlando Morning Sentinel*. Shown here are, from left to right, (first row) W.B. Shiver, R.L. Schacht, manager Bob Potter, unidentified, Tommie Smith, and Harold Morton; (second row) Ellis Starbird, Jimmy Davis, Doug Fielder, Nelson Smith, Vernon Maltby, and Lester Harvey. (Courtesy of the *Orlando Sentinel*.)

The Apopka Little League won the Little League National Championship in 2001. The squad included three members from Zellwood (Will Blankenship, Justin LaFavors, and Andrew Cobb). Shown here are, from left to right, (first row) Blankenship, LaFavors, Cobb, Stuart Tapley, and Beau French; (second row) Josh Tanski, Jeff Lovejoy, Tyler Scanlon, Ryan Markelly, Brandon Brewer, and Zack Zwieg; (third row) Cal Ripkin Jr., coach Bobby Brewer, Ken Tapley, mayor John Land, Pres. George W. Bush, Richard Anderson, Phil Lamphere, and Jack Douglas. (Courtesy of LeRoy and Wanda Brown.)

Erline Bell designed this gown for her 1946 marriage to Wallace "Wally" McCormack. Neighbor Helen Letsinger first made the gown from a sheet. After a fitting, she reproduced it in satin as a gift. Money was tight. Lester Vincent declined a fee for decorating the church, and Mary Vincent served as wedding planner; "Miss Mary" never charged any bride for wedding-planning services. Pianist Evelyn Lovelady learned to play "Clair de Lune" for the wedding. (Courtesy of Erline Bell Chafin.)

A "Tom Thumb wedding" script came to Zellwood with Lydia Hoffman, a teacher from North Dakota who played piano and taught art. The participants pictured here are, from left to right, Sylvia Lister, Ella Mae Rice, Mary Carol Miller, Mary Howard, Peggy Simmons, Gary Potter, Richard Gardner, unidentified, Phillip Simons, Claxton Moore, and Ronnie Gardner. (Courtesy of Mary Wright.)

Martha Letsinger (left), Deloris Brown Lynch (center), and Ann White sang and tap-danced at the birthday party of C.M. Jones, which was held at the Orlando Coliseum on Lake Ivanhoe. The party's attendees were transported by an 18-wheeler. The students of Harriet Jones performed in recitals at the Mount Dora Community Building, Zellwood Community Center, and school talent shows. (Courtesy of the *Orlando Sentinel*.)

This November 3, 1949, image shows the winners of a Youth Center "amateur contest" (as described on the back of the photograph). Pictured here are, from left to right, (first row) Bobby Holloway, Richard Gardner, Gary Potter, Jimmy Hobkirk, Foy C. Wise, Joy Vincent, Mary Agnes Howard, Edna Browning, Harry Bruce, unidentified, and Joan Bartlett; (second row) Glenda Bass, Evelyn Lovelady, Lester B. Vincent Sr., R.E. Haughey, and James A. Vincent. (WL.)

The community put on many plays in the 1980s under the direction of George and Roberta Kluhsmeier. In the above photograph, George (with moustache) poses in front of the cast of *Avalanche of Adversity*. Another popular production was *Hoedown in Corn Town*. George played a role in the Broadway production *South Pacific* before moving to Florida. The below photograph shows the Zellwood Players drama team, which originated in 1998. The team moved their productions to the vintage stage of the Zellwood Community Center in 2010. The outdoor Easter pageant has been held for over a decade at the community center. Zellwood Players consists of local townspeople with a desire to bring family entertainment to surrounding communities. The annual production of *Cricket County*, offering music and the true meaning of Christmas, is a real crowd-pleaser. (Below, courtesy of Hannah Brown Bloser.)

Zellwood exhibited annually at Orlando's Central Florida Fair, claiming blue ribbons, trophies, and regularly winning Best Maintained Booth, an award named after Lester B. Vincent Sr., who was responsible for Zellwood's booth for over 47 years, beginning in 1923. Assembling Zellwood's display became a town-wide volunteer effort undertaken by everyone—from teenagers to octogenarians. Prize money from the fair sustained the community center. Most importantly, the booths showcased Zellwood's wealth of resources. (Courtesy of Evelyn Vincent.)

In this early 1970s image, Mary Whitman Vincent (right) accepts the President's Trophy and the Manager's Blue Ribbon from Pete Parrish (left), president of the Central Florida Fair. The President's Trophy, the highest honor at the Central Florida Fair, was awarded to the Zellwood booth for general excellence and the attractiveness of its homegrown and locally-manufactured products. (Courtesy of Becky Vincent Juvinall.)

In 1946, Zellwood residents wanted to build a youth center, and the town's first fundraiser was the Little Miss Zellwood Contest. Elwood McHaffie placed a photograph of Honey Sheddan in McHaffie's Grocery and collected penny votes, which won Sheddan the crown. Pictured here are, from left to right, (first row) Helen Davenport, Sheddan, and Joann Whitney; (second row) Marjorie Henderson, Julia Fern Haynes, Nellie Ruth Keith, Marguerite Vincent, Sue Elliott, and Daisy Allen. (Courtesy of Honey Sheddan Caldwell.)

Ladies from the Zellwood United Methodist Church gathered for fellowship while creating outstanding quilts. Some of their quilts were sent to the Methodist Children's Home in Enterprise, Florida. Other quilts were given to needy families, and some were sold for funds to continue the worthwhile service. Pictured here are, from left to right, Clifford Vincent Wicker, Byron Morton McCoy, Tessie Morton Owens, Gladys Cooper Vincent, unidentified, Betty Bell, Jessie Goolsby, Dorothy Edwards, and Annie Allen Vincent. (Courtesy of the Vincent family.)

Boy Scout Troop 639 is shown here enjoying a well-deserved camping trip. Zellwood's Boy Scouts have been recognized for their community-improvement projects, including participation in the annual Conquest Cemetery Memorial Day Service, appreciation luncheons each December, numerous work days, and other activities throughout the community. (Courtesy of David Buchan.)

Some Zellwood scouts are pictured here in 2013 during a "Scout Sunday" at Zellwood United Methodist Church, which sponsored this troop. Pictured here are, from left to right, (front row) Jordan McKenna, Kallin Kimball, Adam Kauk, and Jameson McDevitt; (second row) leaders John and Ellen Heizman and Kim McGough; (third row) leader Joe Kauk, Tommy Oh, Zachary McGough, and leader Andre "Andy" Furbush; (fourth row) Dwight Doggett (liaison for scouts and ZUMC), leader John McDevitt, Alex Ameno, leader Nicola McKenna, and Johnson McDevitt. The Eagle Scouts in this picture include Adam Kauk, Kimball, Johnson McDevitt, Zachariah McGough, and Ameno. The Eagle Scouts not pictured are Shaun Buchan, Kyle Yates, Ian Yates, Joseph Heizman, Steven Kauk, and Trevor Furbush. (Courtesy of Hannah Brown Bloser.)

Kay Buchan was the leader of Girl Scout Troop 993 from 1987 through 1999. This group camped at Camp Mah-Kaw-Wee and other venues, including Buchan's backyard in Zellwood. In 1992, these girls rolled Easter eggs on the White House lawn. They are, from left to right, Neecy Gorden Burch, Tonya Holderfield, Bobbi Clark Arbogast, Lauren Choi, Margaret Clark, Jessica Manley, and Janet Buchan Russell. (Courtesy of Kay Buchan.)

The Girl Scout organization has been represented in Zellwood since the early 1920s. In this 1932 image, Girl Scouts pause during a six-mile hike led by troop captain Estelle King. Afterward, they were treated to a weekend of fun and activities hosted by William and Isobel Edwards at their home on the Laughlin Estate. (JFB.)

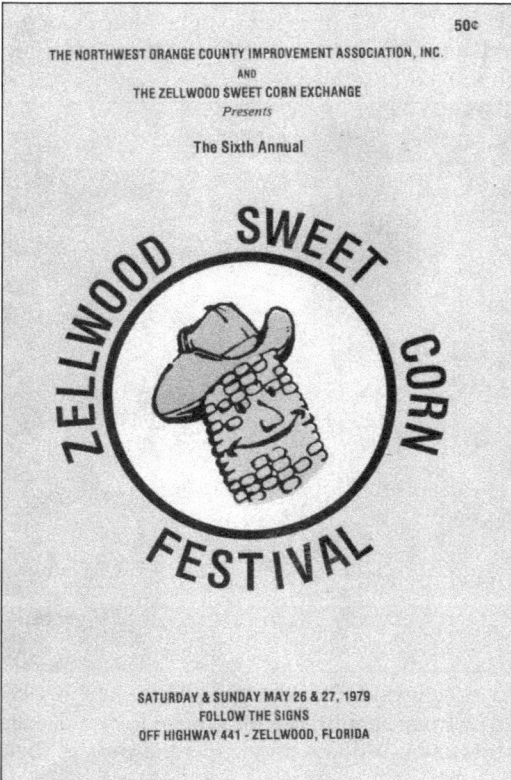

The Northwest Orange County Improvement Association (NOCIA) was organized in 1968 when area residents were concerned about the government rezoning land at the expense of surrounding property owners. That same year, 600 people attended the first NOCIA corn boil, which evolved into the Zellwood Sweet Corn Festival. Each year, the crowd grew larger. John Anderson (above) and other Nashville talents entertain the crowds at the Zellwood Sweet Corn Festival, and arts and crafts vendors remain a huge attraction. NOCIA has made donations over the years to worthwhile organizations whose volunteers worked at the corn festival. (Above, courtesy of NOCIA; left, courtesy of Carol Adkins.)

BMX Action, a California-based magazine, touted Zellwood's BMX practice track as one of the nation's best. In 1983, Tom Miller (pictured)—with help from his father, Paul Miller—started the track with 40 truckloads of clay on a site east of the post office on Zellwood Community Center property. In 1984, Zellwood native Rex Roberson pitched in at the track. BMX professional Todd Corbitt, from Apopka, brought national attention to Zellwood's BMX practice track. (Courtesy of Tom Miller.)

Zellwood Garden Club was federated by the Florida Federation of Garden Clubs in 1960. The club's purposes are to encourage gardening, protect birds, promote conservation, and beautify Florida. The members shown here in the 1990s were given tools as part of the officer installation ceremony. The members are, from left to right, Liz Bragg, Dorothy Jacobus, Sara Eure, Jackie Goins, Sue Hazelwood, Helene Shannon, Rosa Lee Ondich, and Jean Haskins. Annual club activities include decorating the post offices, recognizing home gardeners, planting trees, and holding a Christmas raffle. (Courtesy of Zellwood Garden Club.)

In 1954, concerned citizens raised money to purchase Zellwood's first fire truck, which was parked behind Zellwood Truck Stop. Lester Bill Vincent was the first volunteer fire chief. The fire department was manned entirely by community volunteers. When the alarm sounded, all available men rushed to put out the fire. Later, the volunteer fire department collected money to construct the building shown here. It is still in use today. (Courtesy of Becky Vincent Juvinall.)

In 1993, the Zellwood Community Center dedicated a plaque to commemorate Col. T. Ellwood Zell, principal founder of the Military Order of the Loyal Legion of the United States (MOLLUS). Zell and two "companions" founded MOLLUS in Zell's Philadelphia office while preparing for the funeral cortège of Pres. Abraham Lincoln. Zell was the second person to sign MOLLUS's original document. These "companions" accompanied Lincoln's body on the train to Illinois for burial in 1865. John Philip Sousa wrote "The Loyal Legion March" in honor of MOLLUS. The plaque's location—at the entry of Zellwood Community Center and Zellwood Historical Society, Museum, and Library—is especially appropriate, because Zell was devoted to literary interests. (Courtesy of Dwight Doggett.)

Redlands Christian Migrant Association's Zellwood branch, at 3109 Union Street, opened in 1981. Alma Canahuate, teacher of one- and two-year olds, is pictured here. With twenty teachers, a cook, maintenance workers, and three office workers, RCMA serves children aged two weeks through pre-kindergarten. This nonprofit, nonsectarian organization's program is offered from November through May. (Courtesy of Odemaris Reuter.)

A motorist heading southeast from Jones Avenue on Highway 441 in the 1940s would pass these buildings on the east (upper) side: the post office and Stewart's Sundries building; the two-story mercantile, Bateman's general store and Greyhound bus stop (behind the post office); a rental cottage; a grocery store; Stenstrom's barber shop, a gas station run by Asa Reeves; Claude Jones's Sun State dry-goods store; Rainer's rental cabins and two-story apartments (diagonal to 441); and the Zellwood Coffee Shop. On the west side of Orange Blossom Trail were the train depot, with Leonard Stewart's house behind the depot (lower left), and the Bee Hive (lower right). (Courtesy of Betty Uptagraft.)

Eight

SCHOOLS

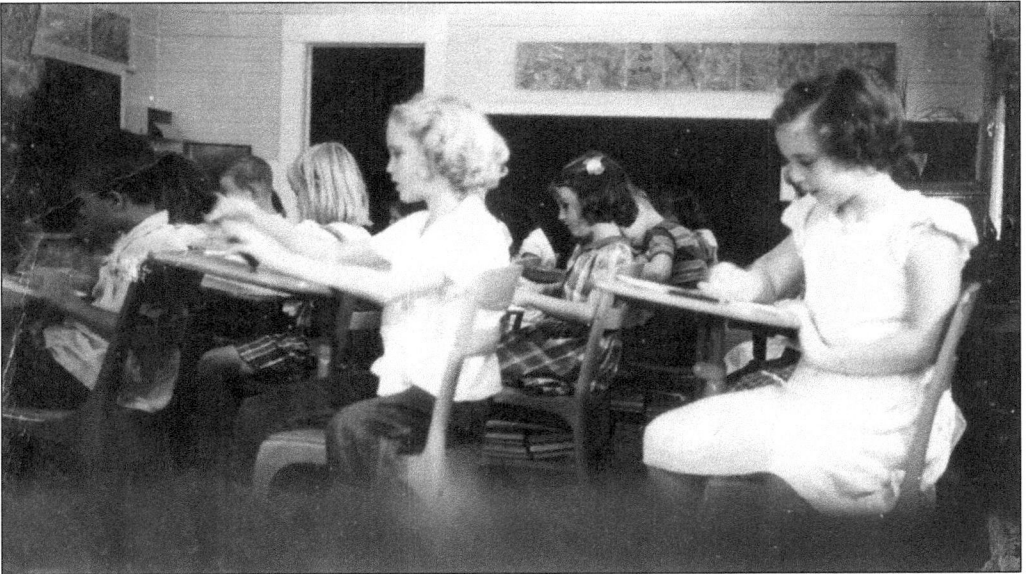

In 1953, Becky Vincent Juvinall (far right) was in the fourth grade at the wooden Zellwood Elementary School. Each year, students anticipated field trips to the symphony at the Orlando Municipal Auditorium (later named the Bob Carr Auditorium). Orange County Public School's itinerant music teacher would bring records and a record player to familiarize students with the year's classical concert selections and to teach them to recognize the instruments of the orchestra. (Courtesy of Becky Vincent Juvinall.)

Zellwood School, located at the top of the hill on King Avenue, was picturesque, with evergreen trees lining each side of the long sidewalk. In the late 1940s and early 1950s, students from music class performed in an annual show with the All County School Chorus in the Orlando Municipal Auditorium. The girls wore white dresses; the boys wore white shirts. Spelling bee finalists attended the yearly spelling bee in Orlando.

In this image from the early 1900s, Americus C. Allen sits front and center with Zellwood students. Professor Allen, who arrived in Zellwood in 1916, was both teacher and principal. At some point, his two daughters—Clarice and Annie Allen—also taught at Zellwood School. (Courtesy of Honey Caldwell.)

The program pictured below is dated May 14, 1915, and indicates that there once was a Zellwood High School whose principal was C.A. Nixon. The five graduating seniors shown in the photograph at right are, in no particular order, Jessie Gardner, Hamilton Jones, Hester Morton, Linna Pike, and Jane Tatlow. (OC.)

The Senior Class
of
The Zellwood High School
requests your presence at their
Graduation Exercises
Friday evening, May the fourteenth
nineteen hundred and fifteen
at eight o'clock
Zellwood High School
Zellwood, Florida

Class Roll

JESSIE GARDNER
HAMILTON JONES
HESTER MORTON
LINNA PIKE
JANE TATLOW

Motto
"Labor omnia vincit."

Colors
Pink and Green

Flower
Sweet Pea

Faculty
PRINCIPAL, C. A. NIXON
Assistants:
MISS WILLIE PEARL HEWGLEY
MISS RUTH MERRILL

From left to right, Lucille Goolsby, Hoss Driver, Louise Goolsby, Glen Morton, and Erline Bell represent the entire 1940 Zellwood Elementary School graduating class. They had attended first through eighth grades at Zellwood and would ride the bus to Apopka High School for the next four years. (Courtesy of Erline Bell Chafin.)

In 1931, nine students graduated from Zellwood Elementary School. In the fall, they would be enrolled in Apopka High School. The students are, from left to right: Gardner McGraw, Helen Stewart, Jerry Svrlinga, Agnes Vincent, Paul Potsko, Mildred Driver, Mike Ondich, Marguerite Hammond, and Amil Bojkovsky. (Courtesy of Rosa Lee Ondich.)

In the 1878 annual report of the St. James Episcopal Mission Church, Reverend Phelps wrote, "I drove to Zellwood and held services in a log school house with temporary floor which also served as town hall, opera house, and church." This image shows the stately new Zellwood School building (which later housed Zellwood Elementary School) with an added library wing, which was donated by J.W. Paul in 1912. The library housed 2,000 volumes donated by Paul and T. Ellwood Zell.

Violet Belle Douglas, a native Floridian, was born in Plant City on October 14, 1901. She attended Stetson University and the Business School of Orlando. Douglas taught elementary students in Zellwood and served as a librarian. She married Leon Osborn in Zellwood in 1940. She was an active member and officer of the Zellwood United Methodist Church, Zellwood Community Center, the Zellwood Library, and a life member of the Zellwood Garden Club. (CVT.)

Erastus "Walter" Fly looks uncharacteristically comical with his necktie askew in this photograph taken around the time he taught upper grades and served as principal at Zellwood Elementary School. After teaching in Zellwood, Fly served as principal of Apopka Junior High School from 1914 through 1917. He taught algebra, geometry, and Latin, and brought the PTA to Apopka. (JFB.)

In 1946, Sally Sewell was the lunchroom manager at Zellwood Elementary School; she is pictured on the far left of the third row. The student to her left is Jean Miller Corbett, who helped in the lunchroom. Sewell was an excellent cook and previously owned a restaurant in Georgia. After leaving the school, she babysat many children in Zellwood while their parents worked. She loved children and taught them high standards. (Courtesy of Jean Corbett.)

After moving from Georgia to Florida, Lois Warren attended college in Tallahassee and Gainesville during the summers. She started teaching after just one year of college. Warren felt inadequately prepared, but she found a teacher's manual published by the state and stayed after school to learn it word for word, which gave her confidence. She taught in Zellwood in the 1940s and later in Union Park, Howey Academy, and Montverde. (Courtesy of Clayton Bishop.)

Three generations of the Fly family were associated with the wooden Zellwood Elementary School on King Street. Erastus "Walter" Fly, who arrived in Zellwood in 1911, served as a teacher and principal. Edwin Fly, Walter's son, attended school there in the 1920s and early 1930s. In the 1950s, Edwin's daughter, Mary Janice Fly (back row, fifth from right), attended first grade at the school with Lois Warren as her teacher. (JFB.)

Through first-grade eyes, Zellwood Elementary School's steps and columns could seemed grandiose and intimidating. This was not the case with the teacher, Marjorie White, with her warm smile. She loved the song "Somewhere Over the Rainbow" and played it often. Her students learned to read that year and enjoyed the playground swings. It was 1951, and the Korean War was going on far away from Zellwood Elementary School. A happy bunch—if they were not the richest kids, they did not seem to know that. (Courtesy of Diana Rice Acree.)

Lydia Hoffman's 1951 fifth-grade class included six students who were advanced to her class from fourth grade: "Skeet" White, George Uptagraft, David Simmons, Horace Weaver, Paul Hobkirk, and Deloris Brown Lynch. History was fun, as the students created dioramas depicting what was taught. Each spring, on May Day, the children would grab crepe paper streamers and dance around the maypole on the playground. (Courtesy of Sheldon Friederich.)

116

The May 1960 photograph above shows sixth graders being promoted in a ceremony at Zellwood Community Center. At that time, Franklin Carver was the principal, and Myrtle Hindmon was the teacher. In addition to the basics, Hindmon taught her class to square dance on Friday afternoons. Many members of this class had previously attended the wooden Zellwood Elementary School, which burned down in 1960. These students were the first sixth graders taught in the concrete building (below), which opened in 1959. Von Nelle Black, Orange County Public Schools' itinerant music teacher, sang "Bless This House" for the new building's dedication. There was no air conditioning or heat in Zellwood Elementary School during the 1959–1960 school year, but each classroom did have a water fountain and a bathroom. The school overlooked Lake Maggiore. (Above, CG; below, courtesy of Zellwood Elementary School.)

This is one of the two 1966 sixth-grade classes at Zellwood Elementary School. In the 1960s, students attending Orange County Public Schools in Zellwood went to Zellwood Elementary for first through sixth grades, then to Apopka Memorial High School for seventh through twelfth grades.

Anna Richardson (standing at far right) taught first, second, and third grades. Her students included Nadine White Starbird and Erline Bell Chafin. While teaching at Zellwood Elementary School, Richardson boarded at the nearby Zellwood Inn. Richardson and Elmer Small Marsell invited Elizabeth Letsinger, proprietress of the Zellwood Inn, to their quiet marriage ceremony. Richardson eventually gave up teaching, and she and her husband made The Old Nest, located on Ponkan Road, their home. (Courtesy of Laurie Marsell.)

118

Laughlin Estate had north, south, east, and west entrances. North Gate was inspired by the city gate of St. Augustine, Florida. In the early 20th century, motorists entering the grounds passed bamboo and moss-laden oaks planted by the estate's 49 gardeners. Years later, the entry road through North Gate was named Dohnavur Drive. Now, parents pass through the historic gates to deliver their children to Hampden DuBose Academy, an interdenominational Christian school. (Courtesy of Twyla Ballard.)

On December 31, 1942, Pierre Wilds DuBose (seated at right, wearing bow tie) purchased 200 acres and approximately 30 buildings on the Laughlin Estate; this would become the campus of Hampden DuBose Academy. In March 1943, approximately 90 students moved from the school's Orlando campus to the Zellwood property. Pictured here are DuBose and his wife, Gwynn, with the faculty, celebrating both James Henderson Cole's return from World War II and the second wedding anniversary of Cole and his wife, Peyton DuBose Cole. (Courtesy of the Orange County Regional History Center.)

In this 1960 photograph, Richard Wolcott (far right) teaches science at Hampden DuBose Academy. The boarding school operated in Zellwood from the 1940s until 1980, with unpaid Christian faculty and staff living in student dormitories on campus. In the fall of 1980, Hampden DuBose Academy became a day school. As of this writing, the school has 125 students, ranging from pre-kindergarten four-year-olds to twelfth-graders, and 25 salaried part- or full-time faculty members. This image is from the school's yearbook, *ESSE*. (Courtesy of *ESSE*.)

The former Laughlin Estate boathouse enhanced Hampden DuBose Academy's waterfront. The school, intent on "Educating for Eternity," emphasized athletic training, sound education, cultural awareness, and spiritual life. At the school's peak, approximately 250 ninth- through twelfth-graders boarded there. Girls wore one-piece bathing suits. Students signed "the pledge," which forbade them from attending movies, smoking cigarettes, drinking alcoholic beverages, or dancing. (Courtesy of Clayton Bishop.)

Nine

RECENT TIMES

In 2013, Hank Scott III (left) and his father, Frank Scott, posed with a 1949 International Harvester Farmall AV tractor on their 1,200-acre sand farm, Long & Scott Farms, Inc. Their triple-sweet corn can be found in Disney restaurants, gourmet specialty markets, and at Scott's Country Market. Their main crop is Great Scott Kirby cucumbers. In 2003, they added a seven-acre corn maze and "agritainment" area to bring more guests to the farm. (Courtesy of Marc Vaughn.)

In March 2012, the Zellwood Community Center (ZCC), led by president Deneth Shiver, partnered with Walt Disney World and KaBOOM! to construct a playground for in Zellwood. Over 100 Disney volunteers and approximately 300 Zellwood-area residents united for the one-day event. Donated breakfasts and lunches for workers were served in Zellwood United Methodist Church's Fellowship Hall. With the leadership of Sohnie Lou Shiver Corder, workers assisted children with activities inside the ZCC while the playground was under construction. Thanks to months of preparation and meetings of various committees, children can now enjoy a new, safe playground. (WL.)

On February 16, 2013, four generations of the families of Billy Long and Frank Scott celebrated 50 years of farming in Zellwood at Long & Scott Farms. Because Long & Scott Farms was on sand land, and not on muck land in the Zellwood Drainage District, the company was not included in the state's muck-farm buyout in 1998. The Scott family continues to grow Scott's Zellwood sweet corn, Great Scott Kirby cucumbers, seedless watermelons, cabbage, and turf grass on their 1,200-acre farm. (Courtesy of Billy Long.)

Birding is increasingly popular in the Lake Apopka Restoration Area, which boasts over 360 species of birds. The first Lake Apopka Wildlife Festival and Birdapalooza was held at Magnolia Park in March 2013. In 2014, an estimated 3,000 people attended the festival, at which birding experts offered walking tours. Buses containing guides from the St. Johns River Water Management District took guests for tours along former farm roads before exiting onto Zellwood's Jones Avenue. (Courtesy of James Peterson.)

After the 1998 buyout of Zellwin Farms' farmland on the Zellwood muck, Zellwin became a produce sales agency with offices in Zellwood and a carrot operation in Georgia. By March 2001, Zellwin was producing egg cartons and trays on Jones Avenue in Zellwood. In its state-of-the-art factory, Zellwin liquefies recycled paper and uses sophisticated machinery to create egg trays and cartons that are imprinted with countless varied labels. (Courtesy of Glenn Rogers.)

In 1981, the Orange County Fire Rescue Department consolidated 13 jurisdictions, including Zellwood. Eighteen to twenty firefighters are assigned to the fire station (No. 20) at 3200 Washington Street, with five on duty at any given time. Station 20 received over 1,100 calls for service in 2013. The station houses Engine 20, Rescue 20, Woods 20, Marine 20, and Tanker 20. Pictured here are, from left to right, Ed Williams, Cory Williams, Mike McCormick, Jerry Hobbs, and Steve Jimmerson. (Courtesy of Donna Hall.)

Zellwood residents united in 1945 to plan the construction of the Zellwood Youth Community Center (now the Zellwood Community Center), which was incorporated in 1946. By February 12, 1947, the building's walls were complete, but the group still needed to raise funds to add the roof. The center was intended to improve the lives of the people of Zellwood by providing a place to socialize. To this day, on the second Tuesday of each month, friends and families meet at ZCC, located at 3160 Union Street, to enjoy a great potluck meal. Each family brings a favorite dish for everyone to eat and enjoy. (Courtesy of Hannah Brown Bloser.)

The current Zellwood post office, located at 3125 North Washington Street in a redbrick building with a Greek Revival entryway, opened in 1976. Leonard "Lenny" Stewart Jr., who served as postmaster in earlier locations since 1935, continued serving until 1978. Samuel T. Adams, postmaster in 2014, stated that there are 770 mailboxes in the current post office, with rural route delivery to 1,255 addresses in Zellwood. (Courtesy of Donna Hall.)

This frame mansion, known as "The White House," was built around 1890 by Jacob W. Paul, who founded Verona Tool Works in 1873. The building now houses the administrative offices of Zellwood Station, an 837-acre adult community located east of Zellwood off of Highway 441. There were 1,131 homes within Zellwood Station in 2014. Its 18-hole golf course is open to both residents and visitors. (Courtesy of Phil Eschbach.)

Sydonie has been part of Zellwood since 1895. Starting in 1904, the mansion was the second home for Pittsburgh steel magnate James Laughlin Jr. In 1942, Hampden DuBose Academy renamed the building Ewell Hall. The academy hosted teas and parties downstairs and used the upper floors as living quarters and a girls' dormitory. In recent years, Dick and Carla Durante and family restored Sydonie to its original grandeur, and it became a private home. (Courtesy of Phil Eschbach.)

During a September 12, 2010, "Celebration of History," the Preservation Advisory Council of the Apopka Historical Society placed 41 local buildings in the Northwest Orange County Register of Historic Places. Pictured here are, from left to right, Angela Nicols, chairman, Preservation Advisory Council; Fred Brummer, Orange County commissioner; Dick Durante, owner of the 1904 Zellwood home Sydonie; Apopka mayor John Land; and Louise Fortunato, cochair, Preservation Advisory Council. (Courtesy of Larry Leudenburg.)

These friends of the Zellwood Historical Society, Museum, and Library volunteered for a Sydonie fundraising event in May 2013. Dick and Carla Durante opened their historic home for tours led by Carla's daughters—Ronda, Jennifer, and Vikki—and friends Penny Nagey and Ellen Heizman. Carla's sister, Imagene Hasson, and museum volunteers hosted this well-attended tour. The effort raised over $9,000 to benefit the Zellwood Historical Society, Museum, and Library, Inc. (Courtesy of Max Horton.)

From left to right, authors Deloris Brown Lynch, Cicily Vincent Turner, Jack Humphrey, Denny Shiver, Marjorie Grinnell, and Rosa Lee Ondich celebrated completion of Images of America: Zellwood by visiting Long & Scott Farms. On behalf of the entire organization, everyone is invited to visit the Zellwood Historical Society's museum in the Zellwood Community Center at 3160 Union Street. Society meetings are held at 7:00 p.m. on the last Thursday of each month. The Facebook page for Zellwood Historical Society is located at www.facebook.com/ZellwoodHistory. (Courtesy of Annette Higgins.)

Visit us at
arcadiapublishing.com